AF303911

Defoe Abbott Marx Hardy Montaigne Machiavelli Chesterton Cooper Emerson Joyce Austen
Melville Carroll Christie Haggard Hugo Eliot Grimm
Stoker Engels Molière
Wilde Maupassant Byron Schiller Kafka
Garnett Fitzgerald Einstein Hawthorne Smith Hall
Goethe Dostoyevsky Willis
Baum Cotton Kipling Doyle
Henry Nietzsche
Leslie Dumas Flaubert Turgenev Balzac
Stockton Vatsyayana Crane
Burroughs Verne
Curtis Tocqueville Gogol Vinci
Homer Widger Tolstoy Whitman Busch
Darwin Thoreau Twain
Potter Freud Zola Scott Plato Harte
Kant Jowett Stevenson Dickens Burton Hesse
Andersen
London Descartes Cervantes Cooke
Poe Aristotle Wells Voltaire
Hale James Hastings
Bunner Shakespeare Cooke
Richter Chekhov Chambers Irving
Doré Dante Shaw da Benedict Alcott
Swift Chekhov Wodehouse Pushkin
Newton

 tredition®

tredition was established in 2006 by Sandra Latusseck and Soenke Schulz. Based in Hamburg, Germany, tredition offers publishing solutions to authors and publishing houses, combined with world-wide distribution of printed and digital book content. tredition is uniquely positioned to enable authors and publishing houses to create books on their own terms and without conventional manu-facturing risks.

For more information please visit: www.tredition.com

TREDITION CLASSICS

This book is part of the TREDITION CLASSICS series. The creators of this series are united by passion for literature and driven by the intention of making all public domain books available in printed format again - worldwide. Most TREDITION CLASSICS titles have been out of print and off the bookstore shelves for decades. At tredition we believe that a great book never goes out of style and that its value is eternal. Several mostly non-profit literature projects provide content to tredition. To support their good work, tredition donates a portion of the proceeds from each sold copy. As a reader of a TREDITION CLASSICS book, you support our mission to save many of the amazing works of world literature from oblivion. See all available books at www.tredition.com.

Project Gutenberg

The content for this book has been graciously provided by Project Gutenberg. Project Gutenberg is a non-profit organization founded by Michael Hart in 1971 at the University of Illinois. The mission of Project Gutenberg is simple: To encourage the creation and distribu-tion of eBooks. Project Gutenberg is the first and largest collection of public domain eBooks.

Women Wage-Earners Their Past, Their Present, and Their Future

Helen Campbell

Imprint

This book is part of TREDITION CLASSICS

Author: Helen Campbell
Cover design: Buchgut, Berlin – Germany

Publisher: tredition GmbH, Hamburg - Germany
ISBN: 978-3-8424-7778-0

www.tredition.com
www.tredition.de

CONTENTS

INTRODUCTION

BY RICHARD T. ELY,

DIRECTOR OF SCHOOL OF ECONOMICS, POLITICAL SCIENCE, AND HISTORY, UNIVERSITY OF WISCONSIN, MADISON.

The importance of the subject with which the present work deals cannot well be over-estimated. Our age may properly be called the Era of Woman, because everything which affects her receives consideration quite unknown in past centuries. This is well. The motive is twofold: First, woman is valued as never before; and, second, it is perceived that the welfare of the other half of the human race depends more largely upon the position enjoyed by woman than was previously understood.

The earlier agitation for an enlarged sphere and greater rights for woman was to a considerable extent merely negative. The aim was to remove barriers and to open the way. It is characteristic of the earlier days of agitation for the removal of wrongs affecting any class, that the questions involved appear to be simple, and easily repeated formulas ample to secure desired rights. Further agitation, however, and more mature reflection always show that what looks like a simple social problem is a complex one.

"If women's wages are small, open new careers to them." As simple as this did the problem of women's wages once appear; but when new avenues of employment were rendered accessible to women, it was found, in some instances, that the wages of men were lowered. A consequence which can be seen in different industrial centres is that a man and a wife working together secure no greater wages than the man alone in industries in which women are not employed. Now, if the result of opening new employments to women is to force all members of the family to work for the wages which the head of the family alone once received, it is manifest that we have a complicated problem.

Another result of wage-earning by women, which has been observed here and there, is the scattering of the members of the family and the break-down of the home. A recent and careful observer among the chief industrial centres of Saxony, Germany, has told us that factory work has there resulted in the dissolution of the family, and that family life, as we understand it, scarcely exists. We have demoralization seen in the young; and in addition to that, we discover that the employment of married women outside the home results in the impaired health and strength of future generations.

The conclusion by no means follows that we should go backward, and try to restrict the industrial sphere of woman. It has been well said that revolutions do not go backward; we have to go farther forward to keep the advantages which have been attained, and at the same time lessen the evils which the new order has brought with it.

Further action is required; but in order that this action may bring desired results, it must be based upon ample knowledge. The natural impulse when we see an evil is to adopt direct methods looking to an immediate cure; but such direct methods which at once suggest themselves generally fail to bring relief. The effective remedies are those which use indirect methods based upon scientific knowledge. If a sympathetic man takes to heart physical suffering, which he can see on every side, he must feel inclined to relieve the distressed at once, and feel impatient if he is hindered in his benevolent impulses; yet we know that he will accomplish far more in the end, if he patiently devotes years to study in medical schools and practice in hospitals before he attempts to give relief to the diseased. We need study quite as much to cure the ills of the social body; and the present work gives us a welcome addition to the positive information upon which wise action must depend.

Mrs. Campbell has been favorably known for years on account of her valuable contributions to the literature of social science, and it gives the present writer great pleasure to have the privilege of introducing this book to the public with a word of commendation.

MADISON, WISCONSIN,

August 29, 1893.

AUTHOR'S PREFACE.

The pages which follow were prepared originally as a prize monograph for the American Economic Association, receiving an award from it in 1891. The restriction of the subject to a fixed number of words hampered the treatment, and it was thought best to enlarge many points which in the allotted space could have hardly more than mention. Acting on this wish, the monograph has been nearly doubled in size, but still must be counted only an imperfect summary, since facts in these lines are in most cases very nearly unobtainable, and, aside from the few reports of Labor Bureaus, there are as yet almost no sources of full information. But as there is no existing manual of reference on this topic, the student of social questions will accept this attempt to meet the need, till more facts enable a fuller and better presentation of the difficult subject.

NEW YORK, *August, 1893.*

WOMEN WAGE-EARNERS;

THEIR PAST, THEIR PRESENT, AND THEIR FUTURE.

INTRODUCTION

The one great question that to-day agitates the whole civilized world is an economic question. It is not the production but the distribution of wealth; in other words, the wages question,—the wages of men and women. Nowhere do we find any suggestion that capital and the landlord do not receive a *quid pro quo*. Instead, the whole labor world cries out that the capitalist and the landlord are enslaving the rest of the world, and absorbing the lion's share of the joint production.

So long as it is a question of production only, there is perfect harmony. Both unite in agreeing that to produce as much as possible is for the interest of each. The conflict begins with distribution. It is no longer a war of one nation with another; it is internecine war, destroying the foundations of our own defences, and making enemies of those who should be brothers.

It is impossible for even the most dispassionate or indifferent observer to blink these facts. Proclaim as we may that there is no antagonism between capital and labor,—that their interests are one, and that conditions and opportunities for the worker are always better and better,—practical thinkers and workers deny this conclusion. Wealth has enormously increased, in a far greater ratio than population. Does the laborer receive his due proportion of this increase? One must unhesitatingly answer no. In a country whose life began in the search for freedom, and which professes to give equal opportunity to all, more startling inequality exists than in any other in the civilized world. One of our ablest lawyers, Thomas G. Shearman, has lately written:—

> "Our old equality is gone. So far from being the
> most equal people on the face of the earth, as we
> once boasted that we were, ours is now the most
> unequal of civilized nations. We talk about the
> wealth of the British aristocracy and about the
> poverty of the British poor. There is not in the
> whole of Great Britain and Ireland so striking a
> contrast, so wide a chasm, between rich and poor
> as in these United States of America. There is no
> man in the whole of Great Britain and Ireland who
> is as wealthy as one of some half-a-dozen men
> who could be named in this country; and there are
> few there who could be poorer than some that
> could be found in this country. It is true that there
> is a larger number of the extremely poor in Great
> Britain and Ireland than there is in this country,
> but it is not true that there is any more desperate
> poverty in any civilized country than ours; and it
> is unquestionably not true that there is any greater
> mass of riches concentrated in a few hands in any
> country than this."

This for America. For England the tale is much the same. "The Bitter Cry of Outcast London," with its passionate demand that the rich open their eyes to see the misery, degradation, and want seething in London slums, is but another putting of the words of the serious, scientific observer of facts, Huxley himself, who has described an East End parish in which he spent some of his earliest years. Over that parish, he says, might have been written Dante's inscription over the entrance to the Inferno: "All hope abandon, ye who enter here." After speaking of its physical misery and its supernatural and perfectly astonishing deadness, he says that he embarked on a voyage round the world, and had the opportunity of seeing savage life in all conceivable conditions of savage degradation; and he writes: —

> "I assure you I found nothing worse, nothing
> more degrading, nothing so hopeless, nothing
> nearly so intolerably dull and miserable as the life I
> left behind me in the East End of London. Were the

alternative presented to me, I would deliberately
prefer the life of the savage to that of those people
in Christian London. Nothing would please me
better — not even to discover a new truth — than to
contribute toward the bettering of that state of
things which, unless wise and benevolent men
take it in hand, will tend to become worse, and to
create something worse than savagery, — a great
Serbonian bog, which in the long run will swallow
up the surface crust of civilization."

In a year and more of continuous observation and study of working conditions in England and on the Continent, some of which will find place later, my own conclusion was the same. The young emperor of Germany, hotheaded, obstinate, and self-willed as he may be, is working it would seem from as radical a conviction of deep wrong in the distributive system. The Berlin Labor Conference, whose chief effort seems to have been against child-labor and in favor of excluding women from the mines, or at least reducing hours, and forbidding certain of the heavier forms of labor, is but an echo of the great dock-strikes of London and the cry of all workers the world over for a better chance. The capitalist seeks to hold his own, the laborer demands larger share of the product; and how to render unto each his due is the great politico-economic question, — the absorbing question of our time.

We have found, then, that the problem is economic, and concerns distribution only. There is no complaint that the capitalist fails to secure his share. On the contrary, even among the well-to-do, deep-seated alarm is evidenced at the rise and progress of innumerable trusts and syndicates, eliminating competition, which restricts production and raises prices. They make their own conditions; drive from the field small tradesmen and petty industries, or absorb them on their own terms.

Rings of every description in the political and the working world combine for general spoliation, and the honest worker's money jingles in every pocket but his own.

Granting all that may be urged as to the capitalists' investment of brain-power and acquired skill, as well as of money with all the risks involved, they are the inactive rather than the active factors in production. They give of their store, while labor gives of its life. Their view is to be reconstructed, and profit-sharing become as much a part of any industry as profit-making.

This is a growing conviction; nor can we wonder that realization of its justice and its possibilities has been a matter of very recent consideration. An often repeated formula becomes at last ingrained in the mental constitution, and any question as to its truth is a sharp shock to the whole structure. We have been so certain of the surpassing advantages of our own country, so certain that liberty and a chance were the portion of all, that to confront the real conditions in our great cities is to most as unreal as a nightmare.

We have conceded at last, forced to it by the concessions of all students of our economic problems, that the laborer does not yet receive his fair share of the world's wealth; and the economic thought of the whole world is now devoted to the devising of means by which he may receive his due. There is no longer much question as to facts; they are only too palpable. Distribution must be reorganized, and haste must be made to discover how.

It is the wages problem, then, with which we are to deal,—the wages of men and women; and we must look at it in its largest, most universal aspects. We must dismiss at once any prejudice born of the ignorance, incompetency, or untrustworthiness of many workers. Character is a plant of slow growth; and given the same conditions of birth, education, and general environment it is quite possible we should have made no better showing. We have to-day three questions to be answered:—

> 1. Why do men not receive a just wage?
> 2. Why are women in like case?
> 3. Why do men receive a greater wage than wom-
> en?

First, Why do not men receive a greater wage than they do? can be answered only suggestively, since volumes may be and have been written on all the points involved. For skilled and unskilled labor alike, the differences in industrial efficiency go far toward regulating the wage, and have been grouped under six heads by General Frances A. Walker, whose volume on the Wages Question is a thoughtful and careful study of the problem from the beginning. These heads are — 1. "Peculiarities of stock and breeding. 2. The meagreness or liberality of diet. 3. Habits voluntarily or involuntarily formed respecting cleanliness of the person, and purity of the air and water. 4. The general intelligence of the laborer. 5. Technical education and industrial environment. 6. Cheerfulness and hopefulness in labor, growing out of self-respect and social ambition and the laborer's interest in his work."

With this in mind, we must accept the fact that the value of the laborer's services to the employer is the net result of two elements, — one positive, one negative; namely, work and waste. Under this head of waste come breakage, undue wear and tear of implements, destruction or injury of materials, the cost of supervision of idle or blundering men, and often the hindrance of many by the fault of one. Modern processes involve so much of this order of waste that often there is doubt if work is worth having or not, and the unskilled laborer is either rejected or receives only a boy's wage.

The various schools of political economists differ widely as to the facts which have formulated themselves in what is known as the iron law of wages; this meaning that wages are said to tend increasingly to a minimum which will give but a bare living. For skilled labor the law may be regarded as elastic rather than iron. For unskilled, it is as certainly the tendency, which, if constantly repeated and so intensified, would end as law. Many standard economists regard it as already fixed; and writers like Lasalle, Proudhon, Bakunin, and Marx heap every denunciation upon it.

Were the fact actually established, no words could be too strong or too bitter to define this new form of slavery. The standard of life and comfort affects the wages of labor, and there is constant effort to make the wage correspond to this standard. It is an unending and often bitter struggle, nowhere better summed up than by Thorold Rogers in his "Six Centuries of Work and Wages," — a work upon which economists, however different their conclusions, rely alike for facts and figures.

We must then admit in degree the tendency of wages to a minimum, especially those of unskilled labor, and accept it as one more motive for persistent effort to alter existing conditions and prevent any such culmination.

Take now, in connection with the six heads mentioned as governing the present efficiency of labor, the five enumerated by Adam Smith in his summary of causes for differences in wages: 1. "The agreeableness or disagreeableness of the employments themselves. 2. The easiness and cheapness, or the difficulty and expense of learning them. 3. The constancy or inconstancy of employment in them. 4. The small or great trust which must be reposed in those who exercise them. 5. The probability or improbability of success in them."

These are conditions which affect the man's right to large or small wage; but all of them presuppose that men are perfectly free to look over the whole industrial field and choose their own employment,—they presuppose the perfect mobility of labor. Let us see what this means.

The theoretical mobility of labor rests upon the assumption that laborers of every order will in all ways and at all times pursue their economic interests; but the actual fact is that so far from seeking labor under the most perfect conditions for obtaining it, nearly half of all humankind are "bound in fetters of race and speech and religion and caste, of tradition and habit and ignorance of the world, of poverty and ineptitude and inertia, which practically exclude them from the competitions of the world's industry."

"Man is, of all sorts of luggage, the most difficult to be transported," was written by Adam Smith long ago; and this stands in the way of really free and unhampered competition. Mr. Frederick Harrison, one of the clearest thinkers of the day, has well defined the difference between the seller and the producer of a commodity. He says:—

> "In most cases the seller of a commodity can send it or carry it from place to place, and market to market, with perfect ease. He need not be on the spot; he generally can send a sample; he usually treats by correspondence. A merchant sits in his counting-room, and by a few letters and forms transports and distributes the subsistence of a

whole city from continent to continent. In other cases, as the shopkeeper, the ebb and flow of passing multitudes supplies the want of locomotion for him. This is a true market. Here competition acts rapidly, fully, simply, fairly. It is totally otherwise with a day laborer who has no commodity to sell. He must himself be present at every market, which means costly, personal locomotion. He cannot correspond with his employer; he cannot send a sample of his strength, nor do employers knock at his cottage door."

It is plain, then, that many causes are at work to depress the wages even of skilled workers, far more than can be enumerated here. If this is true for men, how much more strongly can limitations be stated for women, as we ask, "Why do not women receive a better wage?" Many of the reasons are historical, and must be considered in their origin and growth. Taking her as worker to-day, precisely the same general causes are in operation that govern the wages of men, with the added disability of sex, always in the way of equal mobility of labor.

Wherever for any reason there is immobility of labor, there is always lowering of the wage rate. The trades and general industries for which women are suited are highly localized. They focus in the cities and large towns, and women must seek them there. Great manufactories drain the surrounding country; yet even with these opportunities an analysis of the industrial statistics of the United States by General Walker showed that the women workers of the country made up but seven per cent of the entire population. Eagerly as they seek work, it is far more difficult for them to obtain it than for men. They require to be much more mobile and active in their move toward the labor market, yet are disabled by timidity, by physical weakness, and by their liability to insult or outrage arising from the fact of sex. Men who would secure a place tramp from town to town, from street to street, or shop to shop, persisting through all rebuffs, till their end is accomplished. They go into suspicious and doubtful localities, encounter strangers, and sleep among casual companions. In this fashion they relieve the pressure at congested points, and keep the mass fluid.

For women, save in the slight degree included in the country girl's journey to town or city where cotton or woollen mills offer an opening for work, this course is impossible. Ignorant, fearful, poor, and unprotected, the lions in her way are these very facts. Added to this natural disqualification, comes another,—in the lack of sympathy for her needs, and in the prejudice which hedges about all her movements. In every trade she has sought to enter, men have barred the way. In a speech made before the House of Commons in 1873, Henry Fawcett drew attention to the persistent resistance of men to any admission of women on the same terms with themselves. He said:—

> "We cannot forget that some years ago certain trade-unionists in the potteries imperatively insisted that a certain rest for the arm which they found almost essential to their work should not be used by women engaged in the same employment. Not long since, the London tailors, when on a strike, having never admitted a woman to their union, attempted to coerce women from availing themselves of the remunerative employment which was offered them in consequence of the strike. But this jealousy of woman's labor has not been entirely confined to workmen. The same feeling has extended itself through every class of society. Last autumn a large number of post-office clerks objected to the employment of women in the Post-Office."

Driven by want, they had pressed into agricultural labor as well, and found equal opposition there also. Mr. Fawcett in the same speech calls attention to the fact of the non-admission of women to the Agricultural Laborers' Union, on the ground that "the agricultural laborers of the country do not wish to recognize the labor of women."

There is more or less reason for such feeling. It arises in part from the newness of the occasion, since in the story of labor as a whole, soon to be considered by us in detail, it is only the last fifty years that have seen women taking an active part. We have already seen that mobility of labor is one of the first essentials, and that women are far more limited in this respect than men.

This brings us to the final question, — Why do men receive a larger wage than women? The conditions already outlined are in part responsible, but with them is bound up another even more formidable.

Custom, the law of many centuries, has so ingrained its thought in the constitution of men that it is naturally and inevitably taken for granted that every woman who seeks work is the appendage of some man, and therefore, partially at least, supported. Other facts bias the employer against the payment of the same wage. The girl's education is usually less practical than the boy's; and as most, at least among the less intelligent class, regard a trade as a makeshift to be used as a crutch till a husband appears, the work involved is often done carelessly and with little or no interest. With unintelligent labor wastage is greater, and wages proportionately lower; and here we have one chief reason for the difference. Others will disclose themselves as we go on.

Unskilled labor then, it is plain, must be in evil case, and it is unskilled laborers that are in the majority. For men this means pick and spade at such rates as may be fixed; for women the needle, and its myriad forms of cheap production; and within these ranks is no sense of real economic interest, but the fiercest and blindest competition among themselves. Mere existence is to a large extent all that is possible, and it is fought for with a fury in strange contrast to the apparent worth of the thing itself.

It is this battle with which we have to do; and we must go back to the dawn of the struggle, and discover what has been its course from the beginning, before any future outlook can be determined. The theoretical political economist settles the matter at once. Whatever stress of want or wrong may arise is met by the formula, "law of supply and demand." If labor is in excess, it has simply to mobilize and seek fresh channels. That hard immovable facts are in the way, that moral difficulties face one at every turn, and that the ethical side of the problem is a matter of comparatively recent consideration, makes no difference. Let us discover what show of right is on the economist's side, and how far present conditions are a necessity of the time. It is women on whom the facts weigh most heavily, and whose fortunes are most tangled in this web woven from the beginning of time, and from that beginning drenched with the tears and stained by the blood of workers in all climes and in every age. As women we are bound, by every law of justice, to aid all other women in their struggle. We are equally bound to define the nature, the necessities, and the limits of such struggle; and it is to this end that we seek now to discover, through such light as past and present may cast, the future for women workers the world over.

I.

A LOOK BACKWARD.

The history of women as wage-earners is actually comprised within the limits of a few centuries; but her history as a worker runs much farther back, and if given in full, would mean the whole history of working humanity. The position of working women all over the civilized world is still affected not only by the traditions but by the direct inheritance of the past, and thus the nature of that inheritance must be understood before passing to any detailed consideration of the subject under its various divisions. It is the conditions underlying history and rooted in the facts of human life itself which we must know, since from the beginning life and work have been practically synonymous, and in the nature of things remain so.

In the shadows of that far remote infancy of the world where from cave-dweller and mere predatory animal man by slow degrees moved toward a higher development, the story of woman goes side by side with his. For neither is there record beyond the scattered implements of the stone age and the rude drawings of the cave-dwellers, from which one may see that warfare was the chief life of both. The subjugation of the weaker by the stronger is the story of all time; the "survival of the fittest," the modern summary of that struggle.

Naturally, slavery was the first result, and servitude for one side the outcome of all struggle. Physical facts worked with man's will in the matter, and early rendered woman subordinate physically and dependent economically. The origin of this dependence is given with admirable force and fulness by Professor Lester F. Ward in his "Dynamic Sociology":[1] —

In the struggle for supremacy, "woman at once became property, since anything that affords its possessor gratification is property. Woman was capable of affording man the highest of gratifications, and therefore became property of the highest value. Marriage, under the prevailing form, became the symbol of transfer of ownership, in the same manner as the formal seizing of lands. The passage from sexual service to manual service on the part of women was perfectly natural.... And thus we find that the women of most savage tribes perform the manual and servile labor of the camp."

"The basis of all oppression is economic dependence on the oppressor," is the word of a very keen thinker and worker in the German Reichstag to-day; and he adds: "This has been the condition of women in the past, and it still is so. Woman was the first human being that tasted bondage. Woman was a slave before the slave existed."

Science has demonstrated that in all rude races the size and weight of the brain differ far less according to sex than is the case in civilized nations. Physical strength is the same, with the advantage at times on the side of the woman, as in certain African tribes to-day, over which tribes this fact has given them the mastery. Primeval woman, all attainable evidence goes to show, started more nearly equal in the race, but became the inferior of man, when periods of child-bearing rendered her helpless and forced her to look to him for assistance, support, and protection.

When the struggle for existence was in its lowest and most brutal form, and man respected nothing but force, the disabled member of society, if man, was disposed of by stab or blow; if woman, and valuable as breeder of fresh fighters, simply reduced to slavery and passive obedience. Marriage in any modern sense was unknown. A large proportion of female infants were killed at birth. Battle, with its recurring periods of flight or victory, made it essential that every tribe should free itself from all *impedimenta*. It was easier to capture women by force than to bring them up from infancy, and thus the childhood of the world meant a state in which the child had little place, save as a small, fierce animal, whose development meant only a change from infancy and its helplessness to boyhood and its capacity for fight.

Out of this chaos of discordant elements, struggling unconsciously toward social form, emerged by slow degrees the tribe and the nation, the suggestions of institutions and laws and the first principles of the social state. Master and servant, employer and employed, became facts; and dim suspicions as to economic laws were penetrating the minds of the early thinkers. The earliest coherent thought on economic problems comes to us from the Greeks, among whom economic speculation had begun almost a thousand years before Christ. The problem of work and wages was even then forming, — the sharply accented difference between theirs and ours lying in the fact that for Greek and Roman and the earlier peoples in the Indies economic life was based upon slavery, accepted then as the foundation stone of the economic social system.

Up to the day when Greek thought on economic questions formulated, in Aristotle's "Politics" and "Economics," the first logical statement of principles, knowledge as to actual conditions for women is chiefly inferential. When a slave, she was like other slaves, regarded as soulless; and she still is, under Mohammedanism. As lawful wife she was physically restrained and repressed, and mentally far more so. A Greek matron was one degree higher than her servants; but her own sons were her masters, to whom she owed obedience. A striking illustration of this is given in the Odyssey. Telemachus, feeling that he has come to man's estate, invades the ranks of the suitors who had for years pressed about Penelope, and orders her to retire to her own apartments, which she does in silence. Yet she was honored above most, passive and prompt obedience being one of her chief charms.

Deep pondering brought about for Aristotle a view which verges toward breadth and understanding, but is perpetually vitiated by the fact that he regards woman as in no sense an individual existence. If all goes well and prosperously, women deserve no credit; if ill, they may gain renown through their husbands, the philosopher remarking: "Neither would Alcestis have gained such renown, nor Penelope have been deemed worthy of such praise, had they respectively lived with their husbands in prosperous circumstances; and it is the sufferings of Admetus and Ulysses which have given them everlasting fame."

This is Aristotle's view of women's share in the life they lived; yet gleams of something higher more than once came to him, and in the eighth chapter of the "Economics," he adds: "Justly to love her husband with reverence and respect, and to be loved in turn, is that which befits a wife of gentle birth, as to her intercourse with her own husband." Ulysses, in his address to Nausicaa, says: —

> "There is no fairer thing
> Than when the lord and lady with one soul
> One home possess."

Aristotle, charmed at the picture, dilates on this "mutual concord of husband and wife, ... not the mere agreement upon servile matters, but that which is justly and harmoniously based on intellect and prudence."[2]

Side by side with this picture of a state known to a few only among the noblest, must be placed the lament of "Iphigenia in Tauris":

> "The condition of women is worse than that of
> all human beings. If man is favored by fortune, he
> becomes a ruler, and wins fame on the battlefield;
> and if the gods have ordained him his fortune, he
> is the first to die a fair death among his people. But
> the joys of woman are narrowly compassed: she is
> given unasked, in marriage, by others, often to
> strangers; and when she is dragged away by the
> victor through the smoking ruins, there is none to
> rescue her."

Thucydides, who had already expressed the opinion quoted by many a modern Philistine, — "The wife who deserves the highest praise is she of whom one hears neither good nor evil outside her own house," — anticipates a later verdict, in words that might have been the foundation of Iphigenia's lament: —

> "Woman is more evil than the storm-tossed
> waves, than the heat of fire, than the fall of the

wild cataract! If it was a god who created woman,
wherever he may be, let him know that he is the
unhappy author of the greatest ills."

This was a summary of the Greek view as a whole. Sparta trained her girls and boys alike in childhood; but the theories of Lycurgus, admirable at some points, were brutal and short-sighted at others, and Sparta demonstrated that the extinction of all desire for beauty or ease or culture brings with it as disastrous results as its extreme opposite.

It is Athens that sums up the highest product of Greek thought, and that represents a civilization which from the purely intellectual side has had no successor. Yet even here was almost absolute obtuseness and indifference, on the part of the aristocracy, to the intolerable bondage of the masses. "The people," as spoken of by their historians and philosophers, mean simply a middle class, the humblest member of which owned at least one slave. The slaves themselves, the real "masses," had no political or social existence more than the horses with which they were sent to the river to drink. In any scheme of political economy Aristotle's words, in the first book of the "Politics," were the keynote: "The science of the master reduces itself to knowing how to make use of the slave. He is the master, not because he is the owner of the man, but because he knows how to make use of his property."

In fact, according to this chivalrous philosopher, the man was the head of the family in three distinct capacities; for he says: "Now a freeman governs his slave in the manner the male governs the female, and in another manner the father governs his child; and these have the different parts of the soul within them, but in a different manner. Thus a slave can have no deliberative faculty; a woman but a weak one, a child an imperfect one."

That liberty could be their right appears to have been not even suspected. Yet out from these dumb masses of humanity, regarded less than brutes, toiling naked under summer sun or in winter cold, chained in mines, men and women alike, and when the whim came, massacred in troops, sounded at intervals a voice demanding the liberty denied. It was quickly stifled. The record is there for all to read; stifled again and again, from Drimakos the Chian slave to

Spartacus at Rome, yet each protest from this unknown army of martyrs was one step onward toward the emancipation to come. In each revolution, however small, two parties confronted each other,—the people who wished to live by the labor of others, the people who wished to live by their own labor,—the former denying in word and deed the claim of the latter.

Such conditions, as we proved in our own experience of slavery, benumb spiritual perception and make clear vision impossible; and it is plain that if the mass of workers had neither political nor social place, woman, the slave of the slave, had even less. Her wage had never been fixed. That she had right to one had entered no imagination. To the end of Greek civilization a wage remained the right of free labor only. The slave, save by special permit of the master, had right only to bare subsistence; and though men and women toiled side by side, in mine or field or quarry, there was, even with the abolition of slavery, small betterment of the condition of women. The degradation of labor was so complete, even for the freeman, that the most pronounced aversion to taking a wage ruled among the entire educated class. Plato abhorred a sophist who would work for wages. A gift was legitimate, but pay ignoble; and the stigma of asking for and taking pay rested upon all labor. The abolition of slavery made small difference, for the taint had sunk in too deeply to be eradicated. A curse rested upon all labor; and even now, after four thousand years of vacillating progress and retrogression, it lingers still.

The ancients were, in the nature of things, all fighters. Even when slavery for both the Aryan and Semitic races ended, two orders still faced each other: aristocracy on the one side, claiming the fruits of labor; the freeman on the other, rebelling against injustice, and forming secret unions for his own protection,—the beginning of the co-operative principle in action.

Thus much for the Greek. Turn now to the second great civilization, the Roman. During the first centuries after the founding of Rome the Roman woman had no rights whatever, her condition being as abject as that of the Grecian. With the growth of riches and of power in the State, more social but still no legal freedom was accorded. The elder Cato complained of the allowing of more liberty, and urged that every father of a family should keep his wife in the proper state of servility; but in spite of this remonstrance, a movement for the better had begun. Under the Empire, woman acquired the right of inheritance, but she herself remained a minor, and could dispose of nothing without the consent of her guardian. Sir Henry Maine[3] calls attention to the institution known to the oldest Roman law as the "Perpetual Tutelage of Women," under which a female, though relieved from her parent's authority by his decease, continues subject through life. Various schemes were devised to enable her to defeat ancient rules; and by their theory of "Natural Law," the jurisconsults had evidently assumed the equality of the sexes as a principle of their code of equity.

Few more significant words or words more teeming with importance on the actual economic condition of women have ever been written than those of the great jurist whose name counts as almost final authority. "Ancient law," he writes, "subordinates the woman to her blood relations, while a prime phenomenon of modern jurisprudence has been her subordination to her husband." Under the modified laws as to marriage, he goes on to state, there came a time "when the situation of the Roman female, unmarried or married, became one of great personal and proprietary independence; for the tendency of the later law, as already hinted, was to reduce the power of the guardian to a nullity, while the form of marriage in fashion conferred on the husband no compensating superiority."

These were the final conditions for the Roman, whose power, sapped by long excesses, was even then trembling to its fall. Already the barbarians threatened them, and at various points had penetrated the Empire, showing to the amazed Romans morals absolutely opposed to their own. The German races contented themselves with one wife; and Tacitus wrote of them: "Their marriages are very strict. No one laughs at vice, nor is immorality regarded as a sign of good breeding. The young men marry late,—they marry equal in years and in health, and the strength of the parent is transmitted to the children."

This has a rosier aspect than facts warrant. For the Germans, as for other barbarians of that epoch, the patriarchal family was the social order, and the head of the family the lord of the community.

Wives, daughters, and daughters-in-law were excluded from leadership, though in spite of this there is record of a woman as being occasionally at the head of a tribe,—a circumstance chronicled by Tacitus with much disgust.

While from the West this gigantic wave of powerful but uncultured life was flowing in, from the East had come another. Early Christianity had already established itself, and its ascetic teachings made another element in the contradictions of the time. Up to this date slavery had been the foundation of society, and any amelioration in the condition of women had applied only to the patrician class. The Carpenter of Nazareth set his seal upon the sacredness of labor, and taught first not only the rights but the immeasurable value of even the weakest human soul. Women were ardent converts to the new gospel. Hoping with all the wretched for redemption and deliverance from present evils, they became eager and devoted adherents. Their missionary zeal was a powerful agent in the early days of Christianity. "In the first enthusiasm of the Christian movement," says Principal Donaldson, in his notable article on "Women among the Early Christians," in the "Fortnightly Review," "women were allowed to do whatever they were fitted to do."

All this within a few generations came to an end. Widows of sixty and over retained the power which had been given, and a new order arose,—deaconesses who were not allowed marriage. Neither widows nor deaconesses could teach, the Church being especially jealous in this respect and in substantial agreement with Sophocles, who said, "Silence is a woman's ornament."

Tertullian waxes furious over the thought of a woman learning much, and still more, venturing to use such acquirement; but heretical Christians insisted that the respect which Romans had paid to the Vestal Virgin was her right, and each founder of a new sect had some woman as helper. But as a rule, her highest post during the first three centuries of Christianity was that of doorkeeper or message-woman, her economic dependence upon man being absolute. Social problems remained chiefly untouched. No objection was made to the existence of slavery. In this gospel of love the Christian slave became the brother of all, and kindliness was his right; but their faith demanded contentment with all present ills, since a glorious future was to compensate them. A Christian slave-woman was the property of her master, who had absolute power over her; but no objection seems to have been made to this.

In the mean time many doubts as to marriage seem to have arisen. Paul had set his seal on the subjection of women, and Peter followed suit. Antagonism to marriage grew and intensified, till hardly a Father of the early Church but fulminated against it. Fiercest, loudest, and most heeded of all, the voice of Tertullian still sounds down the ages. This is his address to women:

> "Do you not know that each one of you is an Eve? The sentence of God on this sex of yours lives in this age; the guilt must of necessity live too. You are the devil's gateway; you are the unsealer of that forbidden tree; you are the first deserter of the divine law; you are she who persuaded him whom the devil was not valiant enough to attack. You destroyed so easily God's image, man. On account of your desert, that is, death, even the Son of God had to die."

Clement of Alexandria supplemented this verdict with one as bitter, and Cyprian and the rest echoed the general anathema. As marriage grew thus more and more degraded, the number of the women in the world steadily increased, and posterity in like ratio deteriorated. The summary of Principal Donaldson, in the article already referred to, is the keynote to the whole situation.

> "The less spiritual classes of the people, the laymen, being taught that marriage might be licentious, and that it implied an inferior state of sanctity, were rather inclined to neglect matrimony for more loose connections; and it was these people alone that then peopled the world. It was the survival of the unfittest. The noble men and women, on the other hand, who were dominated by the loftiest aspirations and exhibited the greatest temperance, self-control, and virtue, left no children."

Sir Henry Maine comes to the same conclusion, and deplores the fact of the loss of liberty for women, adding: "The prevalent state of religious sentiment may explain why it is that modern jurisprudence, forged in the furnace of barbarian conquest, and formed by the fusion of Roman jurisprudence with patriarchal usage, has absorbed among its rudiments much more than usual of those rules concerning the position of women which belong peculiarly to an imperfect civilization." And he adds words which come from a man who is a good Christian as well as a profound student: "No society which preserves any tincture of Christian institutions is likely to restore to married women the personal liberty conferred on them by the middle Roman law."

Passing now to the Middle Ages, we find conditions curiously involved. The exaltation of celibacy as the true condition for the religious, and the consequent enormous increase of convents, placed fresh barriers in the way of marriage; and the Church having attracted the gentle and devoted among the women and the more intelligent among the men, the reproduction of the species was for the most part still left to the brutal and ignorant, thus leading to a survival of the unfittest to aid in any advancement of the race.

The number of women far exceeded that of men, who died not only from constant feuds and struggles, but from many pestilences, which naturally, in a day when sanitary laws were unknown, ravaged the country. Dr. Karl Bücher, commenting on the relation of this fact to the life of women at that time, notes that from 1336 to 1400 thirty-two years of plague occurred, forty-two between 1400 and 1500, and thirty between 1500 and 1600. In addition to the convents, which received the well-to-do, many towns established Bettina institutions, houses of God, where destitute women were cared for; but it was impossible for all who sought admittance to be provided for.

The feudal system, with its absolute power over its serfs, had driven thousands into open revolt; and beggars, highwaymen, and robbers made life perilous and trade impossible.

The towns banded together for protection of life and industry, and thus developed the guild of the Middle Ages. Relieved from the fear of free-booting barons, no less dangerous than the hordes of organized robbers, these guilds grew populous and powerful. Licentiousness did not, however, lessen. Luther thundered against it, before his own revolt came; and the Reformation demanded marriage as the right and privilege of a people falsely taught its debasing and unholy nature.

We count the days of chivalry as the paradise of women. Chivalry was for the few, not the many; for the mass of women was still the utter degradation of a barbarous past, and the burden of grinding laws resulting from it. With the Reformation, Germany ceased to be the centre of European traffic; and Spain, Portugal, Holland, and England took the lead in quick succession, England retaining it to the present time. German commerce and trade steadily declined; and as the guilds saw their importance and profits lessen, they made fresh and more stringent regulations against all new-comers. Competitors of every order were refused admission. Heavy taxes on settlement, costly master-examinations, limitations of every trade to a certain number of masters and journeymen, forced thousands into dependence from which there was no escape.

Looking at the time as a whole, one sees clearly how old distinctions had become obliterated. Wealth found new definitions. The Church had made poverty the highest state, and insisted, as she does in part to-day, that the suffering and deprivation of one class were ordained of God to draw out the sympathies of the other. The rich must save their souls by alms and endowments, and contentment and acquiescence were to be the virtues of the poor.

Insensibly this view was modified. Charlemagne, whose extraordinary personal power and common-sense moulded men at will, set an example no monarch had ever set before. He ordered the sale of eggs from his hens and the vegetables from his gardens; and, scorn it as they might, his sneering nobles insensibly modified their own thought and action. Commerce brought the people and products of new countries face to face. The lines of caste, as sharply defined within the labor world as without, were gradually dimmed or obliterated. The practice of credit and exchange, largely the creation of the persecuted Jews, made easy the interchange of commodities. Saint Louis himself organized industry, and divided the trades into brotherhoods, put under the protection of the saints from the tyranny of the barons and of the feudal system which had weighted all industry.

Reform began in the year 1257, in the "Institutions" of Saint Louis,—a set of clear and definite rules for the development of public wealth and the general good of the people. In their first joy at this escape from long-continued oppression, many of the towns of the Middle Ages had admitted women to citizenship on an equal footing with men. In 1160 Louis le Jeune, of France, granted to Theci, wife of Yves, and to her heirs, the grand-mastership of the five trades of cobblers, belt-makers, sweaters, leather-dressers, and purse-makers. In Frankfort and the Silesian towns there were female furriers; along the middle Rhine many female bakers were at work. Cologne and Strasburg had female saddlers and embroiderers of coats-of-arms. Frankfort had female tailors, Nuremburg female tanners, and in Cologne were several skilled female goldsmiths.

Twelve hundred years of struggle toward some sort of justice seemed likely at this point to be lost, for with the opening of the thirteenth century each and all of the guilds proceeded to expel every woman in the trades. It is a curious fact in the story of all societies approaching dissolution, that its defenders adopt the very means best adapted to hasten this end. Each corporation dreaded an increase of numbers, and restricted marriages, and reduced the number of independent citizens. Many towns placed themselves voluntarily under the rule of princes who in turn were trying to subjugate the nobility, and so protected the towns and accorded all sorts of rights and privileges.

The Thirty Years' War, from 1618 to 1648, decimated the German population, and reduced still further the possibility of marriage for many. Forced out of trades, women had only the lowest, most menial forms of trade labor as resort, and their position was to all appearance nearly hopeless.

In spite of this, certain trades were practically woman's. Embroidery of church vestments and hangings had been brought to the highest perfection. Lace-making had been known from the most ancient times; and Colbert, the famous financier and minister for Louis XIV., gave a privilege to Madame Gilbert, of Alençon, to introduce into France the manufacture of both Flemish and Venetian Point, and placed in her hands for the first expenses 150,000 francs.

The manufacture spread over every country of Europe, though in 1640 the Parliament of Toulouse sought to drive out women from the employment, on the plea that the domestic were her only legitimate occupations. A monk came to the rescue, and demonstrated that spinning, weaving, and all forms of preparing and decorating stuffs had been hers from the beginning of time, and thus for a season averted further action.

The monk had learned his lesson better than most of the workmen who sought to curtail woman's opportunities. In the chronicles of that time there is full description of the workshops which formed part of every great estate, that known as the *gynæceum* being devoted to the women and children, who spun, wove, made up, and embroidered stuffs of every order. The Abbey of Niederalteich had such a *gynæceum*, in which twenty-two women and children worked, while that of Stephenswert employed twenty-four; co-operation in such labor having been found more advantageous than isolated work. Before the tenth century these workshops had been established at many points. If part of a feudal manor, the wife of its lord acted often as overseer; if attached to some abbey, a general overlooker filled the same place. In the convents manual labor came into favor; and the spinning, weaving, and dyeing of stuffs occupied a large part of the life.

Apprenticeship for both male and female was finally well established, and many women became the successful heads of prosperous industries. The wage was, as it is to-day, the merest pittance; but any wage whatever was an advance upon the conditions of earlier servitude.

Life had small joy for women in those days we call the "good old times." Take the married woman, the house-mother of that period. She not only lived in the strictest retirement, but her duties were so complex and manifold that, to quote Bebel, "a conscientious housewife had to be at her post from early in the morning till late at night in order to fulfil them. It was not only a question of the daily household duties that still fall to the lot of the middle-class housekeeper, but of many others from which she has been entirely freed by the modern development of industry, and the extension of means of transport. She had to spin, weave, and bleach; to make all the linen and clothes, to boil soap, to make candles and brew beer. In addition to these occupations, she frequently had to work in the field or garden and to attend to the poultry and cattle. In short, she was a veritable Cinderella, and her solitary recreation was going to church on Sunday. Marriages only took place within the same social circles; the most rigid and absurd spirit of caste ruled everything, and brooked no transgression of its law. The daughters were educated on the same principles; they were kept in strict home seclusion; their mental development was of the lowest order, and did not extend beyond the narrowest limits of household life. And all this was crowned by an empty and meaningless etiquette, whose part it was to replace mind and culture, and which made life altogether, and especially that of a woman, a perfect treadmill of labor."

How was it possible that a condition as joyless and fruitless as this should be the accepted ideal of womanhood? Already the question is answered. For ages her identity had been merged in that of the man by whose side she worked with no thought of recompense. She toiled early and late, filling the office of general helper on the same terms; and even to-day, under our own eyes, the wife of many a farmer goes through her married life often not touching five dollars in cash in an entire year.

Submissiveness, clinging affection, humility, all the traits accounted distinctively feminine, and the natural and ever-increasing result of steady suppression of all stronger ones stood in the way of any resistance. Intellectual qualities, forever at a discount, repressed development save in rarest cases. The mass of women had neither power nor wish to protest; and thus the few traces we find of their earliest connection with labor show us that they accepted bare subsistence as all to which they were entitled, and were grateful if they escaped the beating which the lower order of Englishman still regards it as his right to give. Even in our own country and our own time this theory is not altogether extinct. The papers only recently contained an account of the brutal beating of a woman by a man. The woman in remonstrating cried, "You have no right to beat me! I am not your wife!"

During the Middle Ages, and indeed well into the nineteenth century, possession of property by women was confined to the unmarried, the entire control and practical ownership passing to the husband upon marriage.

Change comes at last to even the most fossilized thought. One by one, social institutions clung to with fiercest tenacity fell away. Barbaric independence had followed Greek and Roman slavery, which in turn was succeeded by feudal servitude, to reappear once more in the affranchised communes. Each experiment had its season, and sunk into the darkness of the past, to give place to a new one, which must transmit to posterity the principal and interest of all preceding ones. But though progress when taken in the mass is plain, the individual years in each generation show small trace of it. Even as late as the sixteenth century, the workman fared little better than the brutes. Erasmus tells us that their houses had no chimneys, and their floors were bare ground; while Fortescue, who travelled in France at the same time, reports a misery and degradation which have had vivid portraiture in Taine's "Ancien Régime."

A flood of wealth poured in on the discovery of the New World. The invention of gunpowder put a new face upon warfare, and that of printing made possible the cheap and wide dissemination of long-smouldering ideas. Economic problems perplexed every country, and on all sides methods of solving them were put in action. Sully, who found in Henry IV. of France an ardent supporter of his wishes for her prosperity, had altered and systematized taxes, and introduced a multitude of reforms in general administration; and later, Colbert did even more notable work. The Italian Republics had made their noble code of commercial rules and maxims. The Dutch had given to the world one of the most wonderful examples of what man may accomplish by sheer pluck and persistent hard work, and commercial institutions founded on a principle of liberty; and neither the terror of the Spanish rule nor the jealousy of England had destroyed her power. Credit, banking, all modern forms of exchange were coming into use; and agriculture, which the feudal system had kept in a state of torpor, awakened and became a productive power.

Side by side with this were gigantic speculations, like that of John Law and the East India Company, with the helpless ruin of its collapse. The time was ripe for the formulation of some system of economic laws; and two men who had long pondered them, De Gournay and Quesnay, made the first attempt to explain the meaning of wealth and its distribution. After Quesnay and his system, still holding honorable place, came Turgot; after Turgot, Adam Smith; and thenceforward halt is impossible, and economic science marches on with giant strides.

In all this progress woman had shared many of the material benefits, but her industrial position had altered but slightly. Driven from the trades, she had passed into the ranks of agricultural laborers; and Thorold Rogers, in his "Work and Wages," records her early work in this direction. France held the most enlightened view, and even then women took active part in business, and had a position unknown in any other country; but they had no place in any system of the economists, nor did their labor count as a force to be enumerated. Slowly machinery was making its way, feared and hated by the lower order of workers, eyed distrustfully and uncertainly by the higher. Men and women struggling for bare subsistence had become active competitors, till, in 1789, a general petition entitled "Petition of Women of the Third Estate to the King" was signed by hundreds of French workers, who, made desperate by starvation and underpay, demanded that every business which included spinning, weaving, sewing, or knitting should be given to women exclusively. Side by side with the wave of political revolution, strongest for France and America, came the industrial revolution; and the opening of the nineteenth century brought with it the myriad changes we are now to face.

FOOTNOTES:

[1] Dynamic Sociology, or Applied Social Science as based upon Statical Sociology and the Less Complex Sciences. By Lester F. Ward, A.M., vol. i. p. 649.

[2] Economics, book i. chap. ix.

[3] Ancient Law, p. 147.

II.

EMPLOYMENTS FOR WOMEN DURING THE COLONIAL PERIOD, AND THE DEVELOPMENT OF THE FACTORY.

For nearly a century and a half, dating from the landing of the Pilgrims on Plymouth Rock, the condition of laboring women was that of the same class in all struggling colonies. There were practically no women wage-earners, save in domestic service, where a home and from thirty to a hundred dollars a year was accounted wealth, the latter sum being given in a few instances to the housekeepers in great houses. Each family represented a commonwealth, and its women gave every energy to the crowding duties of a daily life filled with manifold occupations.

The farmer—for all were farmers—was often blacksmith, shoemaker, and carpenter, and more or less proficient in every trade whose offices were called for in the family life. The farmer's wife spun and wove the cloth he wore and the linen that made his household furnishing, and was dyer and dresser, brewer and baker, seamstress, milliner, and dressmaker. The quickness, adaptiveness to new conditions, and the fertility of resource which are recognized as distinguishing the American, were born of the colonial struggle, especially of the final one which separated us forever from English rule.

The wage of the few women found in labor outside the home was gauged by that which had ruled in England. For unskilled labor, as that employed occasionally in agriculture, this had been from one shilling and sixpence for ordinary field work to two shillings a week paid in haying and harvest time. For hoeing corn or rough weeding there is record of one shilling per week, and this is the usual wage for old women. To this were added various allowances which have gradually fallen into disuse. A full record of these and of rates in general will be found in "Six Centuries of Work and Wages."[4]

Unskilled labor during the whole colonial period — meaning by this such labor as that of the men who sawed wood, dug ditches, or mended roads, mixed mortar for the mason, carried boards to the carpenter, or cut hay in harvest time — brought a wage of seldom more than two shillings a day, fifteen shillings a week making a man the envy of his fellows, while six or seven was the utmost limit for women of the same order.

On this pittance they lived as they could. Sand did duty as carpet for the floor. The cupboard knew no china, and the table no glass. Coal and matches were unknown; they had never seen a stove. The meals of coarsest food were eaten from wooden or pewter dishes. Fresh meat was seldom eaten more than once a week. A pound of salt pork was tenpence, and corn three shillings a bushel. Clothing was as coarse as the food, and imprisonment for the slightest debt was the shadow hanging over every family where illness or any other cause had hindered earning. Boys and girls in the poorer families were employed by the owners of cattle to watch and keep them within bounds, countless troubles arising from their roaming over the unfenced fields. Andover, Mass., being from the beginning of a thrifty turn of mind, passed, soon after the founding of the town, an ordinance which still stands on the town records: —

> "The Court did herupon order and decree that in
> every towne the chosen men are to take care of
> such as are sett to keep cattle, that they may be sett
> to some other employment withall, as spinning
> upon the rock, knitting and weaving tape, &c."

Spinning-classes were also formed; the General Court of Massachusetts ordering these in 1656, this being part of the general effort to begin some form of manufactures. But fishing to load ships, and shipbuilding to carry cured fish absorbed the energies of the growing population; and these vessels brought textiles and manufactured goods from the cheapest markets everywhere and anywhere.[5]

These "homespun" industries soon showed a tendency toward division. By 1669 much weaving was done outside the home as custom work; and there is record of one Gabriel Harris who died in 1684 leaving four looms and tacklings and a silk loom as part of the small fortune he had accumulated in this way.[6] His six children and some hired women assisted in the work. In 1685 Joseph, the son of Roger Williams, entered in an account book now extant,[7] a credit to "Sarah badkuk [Babcock], for weven and coaming wisted." This work was, however, chiefly in the hands of men.

The records of Pepperell, Mass., show that many women saved their pin money, and sent out little ventures in the ships built at home and sailing to all ports with fish. These ventures included articles of clothing, embroideries, and anything that it seemed might be made to yield some return. There were also women of affairs, some of whom took charge of large industries. Thus Weeden, in his "Economic and Social History of New England," quotes from an interesting memorandum left by Madam Martha Smith, a widow of St. George's Manor, Long Island,[8] which shows her practical ability. In January, 1707, "my company" killed a yearling whale, and made twenty-seven barrels of oil. The record gives her success for the year, and the tax she paid to the authorities at New York,—fifteen pounds and fifteen shillings, a twentieth part of her year's gains.

Other women oversaw the curing of the fish; but there is no record of the wage beyond the general one which for the earliest days of the colony gives rates for women as from four to eight pence a day without food. These rates followed almost literally those of England at that time. Half of the day's earnings were accounted an equivalent for diet, and contractors for feeding gangs in agriculture, among sailors, or wherever the system was adopted, allowed seven and one-half pence per day a head for men and women alike. Women servants received ten shillings a year wages, and an allowance of four shillings additional for clothing. The working day still remained as fixed by the law late in the fifteenth century,—from five A.M. to eight P.M., from March to September, with half an hour for breakfast, and an hour and a half for dinner.

These rates gradually altered, but for women hardly at all, the wages during the eighteenth century ranging from four to six pounds a year. The colony, however, gave opportunities unknown to the mother country, and gardening and the cultivation of small vegetables seem to have fallen much into the hands of women.[9]They had studied the best methods for hotbeds, and grew early vegetables in these, the first record of this being in 1759.

Gloves were by this time made at home, buttons covered, and many small industries conducted, all connected with the manufacture and making up of clothing. Patriotic spinning occupied many; and the "Boston News-Letter" has it that often seventy linen-wheels were employed at one gathering. The agitation caused by the Stamp Act turned the attention of all women to the production of cloth as a domestic business. Worcester, Mass., in 1780 formed an association for the spinning and weaving of cotton, and a jenny was bought by subscription.[10]

Prices by this time had risen, and in 1776 the Andover records mention that a Miss Holt was paid eighteen shillings for spinning seventy-two skeins, and seven shillings eleven pence for weaving nineteen yards of cloth. Women generally could spin two skeins of linen yarn a day; but there is record of one, a Miss Eleanor Fry of East Greenwich, R.I., who spun seven skeins and one knot in one day,—an amount sufficient to make twelve large lawn handkerchiefs such as were then imported from England.

Within four years another Rhode Island family of Newport are recorded in 1768 as having "manufactured nine hundred and eighty yards of woolen cloth, besides two coverlids (coverlets), and two bed-ticks, and all the stocking yarn of the family."

The Council of East Greenwich fixed prices at that time at rates which seem purely arbitrary and are certainly incomprehensible. Thus for spinning linen or worsted, five or six skeins to the pound, the price was not to exceed sixpence per skein of fifteen knots, with finer work in proportion. Carded woollen yarn was the same per skein. Weaving plain flannel or tow or linen brought fivepence per yard; common worsted and linen, one penny a yard; and other linens in like proportion.[11]

Silk growing and weaving had been the result of the silkworm cocoons sent over by James the First, who offered bounties of money and tobacco for spun and woven silk according to weight. Three women were famous before the Revolution as silk growers and weavers,—Mrs. Pinckney, Grace Fisher, and Susanna Wright; and at all points where the mulberry-tree was indigenous or could be made to grow, fortune was regarded as assured. The project failed; but the efforts then made paved the way for present experiment, and even better success than that already attained.

The manufacture of straw goods, amounting now to many million dollars yearly, owes its origin to a woman,—Miss Betsey Metcalf, who in 1789, when hardly more than a child, discovered the secret of bleaching and braiding the meadow grass of Dedham, her native town. Others were taught, and a regular business of supplying the want for summer hats and bonnets was organized, and has grown to its present large proportions.

At this period women widowed by the fortune of war or forced by the absence of all the male members of the family on the field, were often found in business. The mother of Thomas Perkins of Salem, one of the great American merchants, left widowed in 1778, took her husband's place in the counting-house, managed business, despatched ships, sold merchandise, wrote letters, all with such commanding energy that the solid Hollanders wrote to her as to a man.[12] The record of one day's work of Mary Moody Emerson, born in 1777, reads:—

> "Rose before light every morn; read Butler's Analogy; commented on the Scriptures; read in a little book Cicero's Letters—a few touches of Shakespeare—washed, carded, cleaned house and baked."[13]

There is another woman no less busy, a member of the distinguished Nott family, who did work in her house and helped her boys in the fields. In midwinter, with neither money nor wool in the house, one of the boys required a new suit. The mother sheared the half-grown fleece from a sheep, and in a week had spun, wove, and made it into clothing, the sheep being protected from cold by a wrappage made of braided straw.

Details like this would be out of place here did they not serve to accent the fact of the concentration of industries under the home roof, and the necessity that existed for this. But a change was near at hand, and it dates from the first bale of cotton grown in the country.

In the early years of the eighteenth century not a manufacturing town existed in New England, and for the whole country it was much the same. A few paper-mills turned out paper hardly better in quality than that which comes to us to-day about our grocery packages. In a foundry or two iron was melted into pigs or beaten into bars and nails. Cocked hats and felts were made in one factory. Cotton was hardly known.[14] De Bow, in his "Industrial Resources of the United States," tells us that a little had been sent to Liverpool just before the battle of Lexington; but linen took the place of all cotton fabrics, and was spun at every hearth in New England.

In the eight bales of cotton, grown on a Georgia plantation, sent over to Liverpool in 1784, and seized at the Custom House on the ground that so much cotton could not be produced in America, but must come from some foreign country, lay the seed of a new movement in labor, in which, from the beginning, women have taken larger part than men. By 1800 cotton had proved itself a staple for the Southern States, and even the second war with England hardly hindered the planters. In 1791 two million pounds had been raised; in 1804 forty-eight million; the invention of the cotton-gin, in 1793, stimulating to the utmost the enthusiasm of the South over this new road to fortune.

It is with the birth of the cotton industry that the work and wages of women begin to take coherent shape; and the history of the new occupation divides itself roughly into three periods. The first includes the ten or fifteen years prior to 1790, and may be called the experimental period; the second covers the time from 1790 to 1811, in which the spinning-system was established and perfected; and the third the years immediately following 1814, in which came the introduction of the power loom and the growth of the modern factory system.

The experimental stage found an enthusiastic worker in the person of Tench Coxe, known often as the "Father of American Industries," whose interest in the beginning was philanthropic rather than commercial. Bent upon employment for idle and destitute workmen, he exhibited in Philadelphia in 1775 the first spinning-jenny seen in America. He had already incorporated the "United Company of Philadelphia for Promoting American Manufactures," and they at once secured the machine and made ready to operate it. Four hundred women were very speedily at work at hand spinning and weaving; and though the company presently turned its attention to woollen fabrics, a large proportion of women was still employed.

Till the building of the great mill at Waltham, Mass., in which every form of the improved machinery found place, spinning was the only work of the factories. All the yarn was sent out among the farmers to be woven into cloth, the current prices paid for this being from six to twelve cents a yard. American cotton was poor, and the product of a quality inferior to the coarsest and heaviest-unbleached of to-day; but experiment soon altered all this.

To manufacture the raw product in this country was a necessity. For England this had begun in 1786; but she guarded so jealously all inventions bearing upon it that none found their way to us. Our machinery was therefore of the most imperfect order, the work chiefly of two young Scotch mechanics. In 1788 a company was formed at Providence, R.I., for making "homespun cloth," their machinery being made in part from drawings from English models. Carding and roving were all done by hand labor; and the spinning-frame, with thirty-two spindles, differed little from a common jenny, and was worked by a crank turned by hand.

Even at this stage England was determined that America should have neither machinery nor tools, and still held to the act passed in 1789 which enforced a penalty of five hundred pounds for any one who exported, or tried to export, "blocks, plates, engines, tools, or utensils used in or which are proper for the preparing or finishing of the calico, cotton, muslin, or linen printing manufacture, or any part thereof."

Nothing could have more stimulated American invention; but there were many struggles before the thought finally came to all interested, that it might be possible to condense the whole operation with all its details under one roof, — a project soon carried out.

Thus far all had been tentative; but the building in 1790 at Pawtucket, R.I., of the first large factory with improved machinery gave the industry permanent place. Another mill was erected in the same State in 1795, and two more in Massachusetts in 1802 and 1803. In the three succeeding years ten more were built in Rhode Island and one in Connecticut, altogether fifteen in number, working about 8,000 spindles and producing in a year some 300,000 pounds of yarn. At the end of the year 1809 eighty-seven additional mills had been put up, making about 80,000 spindles in operation. Eight hundred spindles employed forty persons, — five men and thirty-five women and children.

The first authoritative record as to the progress of the manufacture, numbers employed, etc., was made in a report to the House of Representatives in the spring session of 1816. In the previous year 90,000 bales had been manufactured as against 1,000 in 1800. The capital invested was $40,000, and the relative number of males and females employed is also recorded, —

Males employed from the age of 17 and upward	10,000
Women and female children	66,000
Boys under 17 years of age	24,000

For these women spinning was the only work. Hand-looms still did all the weaving, nor was it possible to obtain any plan of the power looms, — then in use in England, and a recent invention. Another mill had been built in 1795; and thus the first definite and profitable occupation for women in this country dates back to the close of the eighteenth and the early years of the nineteenth century, the history of its phases having been written by Tench Coxe. The village tailoress had long gone from house to house, earning in the beginning but a shilling a day, and this sometimes paid in kind; and in towns a dressmaker or milliner was secure of a livelihood. But work for the many was unknown outside of household life; and thus wage rates vary with locality, and are in most cases inferential rather than matter of record.

Cotton would seem, from the beginning of manufacturing interests, to have monopolized New England; but other industries had been very early suggested. In May, 1640, the General Court of Massachusetts made an order for the encouragement by bounties of the manufacture of linen and woollen as well as cotton. In 1638 a company of Yorkshiremen came over and settled in Rowley, Mass., where they built the first fulling-mill in the United States. Fustians and the ordinary homespun cloth were woven; but few women were employed, the work being far heavier than the weaving of cotton. It was hoped that broadcloths as good as those imported could be made; but American wool proved less susceptible of high finish, though of better wearing quality than the English. Various grades of cloth, with shawls, were manufactured; but the growth of the industry was slow, and constantly hampered by heavy duties and much interference. In 1770 the entire graduating class at Harvard College were dressed in black broadcloth made in this country, the weaving of which had been done in families. Yarn was sent to these after the wool had been made ready in the mills, and the census of the United States for 1810 gives the number of yards woven in this way as 9,528,266.

What proportion of women were engaged we have no means of knowing; but the census of 1860 shows that New England had 65 per cent of the total number then at work. The cotton manufacture had but 38 per cent of males as against 62 per cent of females; while in woollen, males were 60 per cent. In New England 10,743 women were in woollen-mills; in the Middle States, 4,540; and in the South, 689. For the West no returns are given. Many more would be included in the Southern returns were it not that most of the weaving is still a home industry, this resulting from the sparseness and scattered nature of the population.

Knitting formed one of the earliest means of earning for women, the demand for hose of every description being beyond the power of the family to supply. Knitting-machines of various orders were in use on the Continent, and had been brought into England; but any attempt to employ them here was for a long time unsuccessful. Yarn was spun especially for this purpose, usually with a double thread, and in the year 1698 Martha's Vineyard exported 9,000 pairs. The German and English settlers of Pennsylvania brought many hand-knitting machines with them, and were rivals of New England; but Virginia led, and the census of 1810 credits her with over half of the hand-knit pairs exported, Connecticut coming next. In Pennsylvania the women earned half a crown a pair for the long hose, and this in the opening of the eighteenth century; and the State still retains it as a household industry. The percentage for the United States of women engaged in it by the last census is 61,100.

The early stages of the industry employed very few women, the processes involving too heavy labor; and out of 159 workers in the first mills, only eight were women, these being employed in carding and fulling. According to our last census, 10,743 are employed in New England mills alone; but the proportion remains far below that of the cotton-mills, and at many points in the South and remote territories it is still a household industry in which all share.

Until well on in the nineteenth century the factory and the domestic system were still interwoven, nor had there been intelligent definition of the actual meaning of this system until Ure formulated one: —

> "The factory system in technology is simply the combined operation of many orders of work-people in tending with assiduous skill a series of productive machines, continuously impelled by a central power."[15]

A central power controlling an army of workers had been the dream of all mechanicians; and Ure formulated this also: —

> "It is the idea of a vast automaton, composed of various mechanical and intellectual organs, acting in uninterrupted concert for the production of a common object, — all of them being subordinate to a self-regulated moving force."

This was the result brought about by the gradual extension of the factory system. The objections made from the beginning, and still made, with such answers as experience has suggested, find place later on.

FOOTNOTES:

[4] By Thorold Rogers.

[5] Weeden's Economic and Social History of New England, vol. i. p. 304.

[6] Caulkins, p. 273.

[7] Rider's Book Notes, vol. ii. p. 7.

[8] Boston News-Letter, Jan. 25, 1773.

[9] Boston News-Letter, Jan. 25, 1773.

[10] Barry's Massachusetts, vol. xi. p. 193.

[11] Weeden's Social and Economic History of New England, vol. ii. p. 790.

[12] Proceedings of the Massachusetts Historical Society, 1798-1835, p. 353.

[13] Atlantic Monthly, December, 1883, p. 773.

[14] For further detail, see McMaster's History of the United States, vol. i. p. 62.

[15] Philosophy of Manufactures, by Andrew Ure, M.D., p. 13.

III.

EARLY ASPECTS OF FACTORY LABOR FOR WOMEN.

Lack not only of machinery but of any facilities for its manufacture hampered and delayed the progress of the factory movement in the United States; but these difficulties were at last overcome, and in 1813 Waltham, Mass., saw what is probably the first factory in the world that combined under one roof every process for converting raw cotton into finished cloth.

Manufacturing, even when most hampered by the burden of taxation then imposed and the heavy duties and other restrictions following the long war, began under happier conditions than have ever been known elsewhere. Unskilled labor had smallest place, and of this class New England had for long next to no knowledge. Her workers in the beginning were recruited from the outlying country; and the women and girls who flocked into Lowell, as in the earliest years they had flocked into Pawtucket, were New-Englanders by birth and training. This meant not only quickness and deftness of handling, but the conscientious filling of every hour with the utmost work it could be made to hold.

The life of the Lowell factory-girls has full record in the little magazine called the "Lowell Offering," published by them for many years. Lucy Larcom has also lately given her "Recollections," one of the most valuable and characteristic pictures of the life from year to year, and it tallies with the summary made by Dickens in his "American Notes." Beginning as a child of eleven, whose business was simply to change bobbins, she received a wage of one dollar a week, with one dollar and a quarter for board, the allowance made by most of the corporations while the system of boarding-houses in connection with the factories lasted. The oldest corporation, known as the Merrimack, introduced this system, and for many years retained oversight of all in its employ. With increasing competition and the increase of the foreign element, alteration of methods began, and Lowell lost its characteristic features.

In the beginning the conditions of factory labor for New England at the point where work was initiated, were, as compared with those of England, almost idyllic. The Lowell workers came from New England farms, many of them for the sake of being near libraries and schools, and thus securing larger opportunities for self-culture.

The agricultural class then outranked merchants and mechanics. There were no class distinctions, and the workers shared in the best social life of Lowell. The factory was an episode rather than a career; and the buildings themselves were kept as clean as the nature of the work admitted, growing plants filling the windows; and the swift-flowing Merrimac turning the wheels.

In 1841 the girls had to their credit in the savings-banks established by the corporations over one hundred thousand dollars; and many of them shared their earnings with brothers who sought a college education, or lifted the mortgages on the home farms. At the International Council of Women, held in Washington in 1888, Mrs. H.H. Robinson, after telling how she entered the Lowell Mills as a "doffer," when a child, gave a brilliant description of the intellectual life and interests of the workers. She remained in the mill till married, and said: "I consider the Lowell Mills as my *alma mater*, and am as proud of them as most girls of the colleges in which they have been educated."

With the growth of the factory system under very different conditions from that of Lowell, there were as different results. Factories had risen, at every available point in New England, all of them thronged by women and girls. But great cities were still unknown; and the first census, that for 1790, showed that hardly four per cent of the people were in them. The tide set toward the factory towns as strongly as it now does toward the cities, though factory labor for the most part was of almost incredible severity. The length of a day's labor varied from twelve to fifteen hours, the mills of New England running generally thirteen hours a day the year round. Several mills are on record, the day in one of which was fourteen hours, and in the other fifteen hours and ten minutes, this latter being the Eagle Mill at Griswold, Conn.; and previous to 1858 there were many others where hours were equally long. Work began at five in the morning, or at some points a little later; and there is a known instance of a mill in Paterson, N.J., in which women and children were required to be at work by half-past four in the morning.

In most of the New England factories, the operatives were taxed for the support of religion. The Lowell Company dismissed them if often absent from church, and their lives without and within the factory were regulated as minutely as if in the cloister. Women and children were urged on by the cowhide; and the first inspection of the factories, notably in Connecticut, revealed a state of things hardly less harrowing than that which had brought about the passage of the first Factory Acts in England. At the same time wages were very inadequate. In twelve hours' daily labor the weavers of Baltimore were able to earn from sixty to seventy cents a day, the wage of the women being half or a third this amount; and they declared it not enough to pay the expenses of schooling for the children.

With the increase of production and the growing competition of manufacturers, wages were steadily forced downward. Less and less attention was paid to the comfort or well-being of the operatives, and many factories were unfit working-places for human beings. Overseers, whose duty it was to keep up the utmost rate of speed, flogged children brutally; and the treatment was so barbarous that a boy of twelve at Mendon, Mass., drowned himself to escape factory labor. Windows were often nailed down, and their raising forbidden even in the hottest weather.

The most formidable and trustworthy arraignment of these conditions is to be found in a pamphlet printed in 1834, the full title of which is as follows: "An Address to the Working-men of New England, on the State of Education, and on the Condition of the Producing Classes in Europe and America."

The author of this pamphlet, a mechanic of some education, stirred to the heart by the abuses he saw, made an exhaustive examination of the New England mills; and he gives many details of the hours of labor, the wages of employees, and the abuses of power which he found everywhere among unscrupulous manufacturers. The principal value of his work lies in this, and in his reprint of original documents like the "General Rules of the Lowell Manufacturing Company," and "The Conditions on which Help is hired by the Cocheco Manufacturing Company, Dover, N.H." These conditions were so oppressive that in several cases revolt took place,— usually unsuccessful, as no organization existed among the women, and they were powerless to effect any marked change for the better.

By 1835 chiefly the poorer order of workers filled the mills, but even skilled labor made constant complaint of cruelties and injustices. Not only were there distressing cases of cruelty to children, but outrage of every kind had been found to exist among the women workers, whose wage had been lowered till nearly at the point known to-day as the subsistence point. Parents then, as now, gave false returns of age, and caught greedily at the prospect of any earning by their children; and any specific enactments as to schooling, etc., were still delayed.

These evils were not confined to New England, but existed at every point where manufacturing was carried on. But New England was first to decide on the necessity for some organized remonstrance and resistance, and the first meeting to this end was held in February, 1831. Of this there is no record; but the second, held in September, 1832, is given in the first "Report of the Massachusetts Bureau of Labor," issued in 1870. Boston sent thirty delegates, and the workingmen of New York City addressed a letter to the workers of the United States, showing that the same causes of unrest and agitation existed at all points.

"These evils," they said, "arise from the moral obliquity of the fastidious, and the cupidity of the avaricious. They consist in an illiberal opinion of the worth and rights of the laboring classes, an unjust estimation of their moral, physical, and intellectual powers, and unwise misapprehension of the effects which would result from the cultivation of their minds and the improvement of their condition, and an avaricious propensity to avail of their laborious services, at the lowest possible rate of wages for which they can be induced to work."

The evils protested against here did not lessen as time went on. Irish emigration had begun in 1836, and speedily drove out American labor, which was in any case insufficient for the need. A lowered wage was the immediate consequence, the foreigner having no standard of living that included more than bare necessaries. At this distance from the struggle it is easy to see that the new life was educational for the emigrant, and also forced the American worker into new and often broader channels. But for those involved such perception was impossible, and the new-comers were regarded with something like hatred. English and German emigrants followed, to give place in their turn to the French-Canadian, who at present in great degree monopolizes the mills.

In the beginning little or no effort was made toward healthful conditions of work and life, or more than the merest hint of education. England, in which far worse conditions had existed, had, early in the century, seen the necessity of remedial legislation. But though the first English Factory Act was passed in 1802, it was not till 1844 that women and children were brought under its provisions. The first one, known as the Health and Morals Act, was the result of the discovery made first by voluntary, then by appointed inspectors, that neither health nor morals remained for factory-workers, and that hopeless deterioration would result unless government interfered at once. Hideous epidemic diseases, an extinction of any small natural endowment of moral sense, and a daily life far below that of the brutes, had showed themselves as industries and the attendant competition developed; and the story in all its horror may be read in English Bluebooks and the record of government inspectors, and made accessible in the works of Giffen, Toynbee, Engels, and other names identified with reform.

The bearing of these acts upon legislation in our country is so strong that a summary of the chief points must find mention here. In the Act of 1802 the hours of work, which had been from fourteen to sixteen hours a day, were fixed at twelve. All factories were required to be frequently whitewashed, and to have a sufficient number of windows, though these provisions applied only to apprenticed operatives. In 1819 an act forbade the employment of any child under nine years of age, and in 1825 Saturday was made a half-holiday. Night work was forbidden in 1831, and for all under eighteen the working day was made twelve hours, with nine for Saturday.

By 1847 public opinion demanded still more change for the better, and the day was made ten hours for working women and young persons between thirteen and eighteen years, though they were allowed to work between six A.M. and six P.M., with an allowance of an hour and a half at mealtime. Our own evils, while in many points far less, still were in the same direction. Here and there a like evasion of responsibility and of the provisions of the law was to be found. Even when a corps of inspectors were appointed, they were bribed, hoodwinked, and generally put off the track, while the provisions in regard to the shielding of dangerous machinery, cleanliness, etc., were ignored by every possible method. Were law obeyed and its provisions thoroughly carried out, English factory operatives would be better protected than those of any other country, America not accepted. Sanitary conditions are required to be good.

All factories are to be kept clean, as any effluvia arising from closets, etc., renders the owners liable to a fine. The generation of gas, dust, etc., must be neutralized by the inventions for this purpose, so that operatives may not be harmed thereby. Any manufacturer allowing machinery to remain unprotected is to be prosecuted; and there are minute regulations forbidding any child or young person to clean or walk between the fixed and traversing part of any self-acting machine while in motion. At least two hours must be allowed for meals, nor are these to be taken in any room where manufacturing is going on.

For this country such provisions were long delayed, nor have we even now the necessary regulations as to the protection of machinery. In the early days, though many mills were built by men who sought honestly to provide their employees with as many alleviations as the nature of the work admitted, many more were absolutely blind to anything but their own interest. With the disabilities resulting we are to deal at another point. It is sufficient to say here, that the struggle for factory-workers became more and more severe, and has remained so to the present day.

The increase of women workers in this field had been steady. In 1865 women operatives in the factories of Massachusetts were 32,239, or nineteen per cent of men operatives. In 1875 they were 83,207, or twenty-six per cent; and the increase since that date has been in like proportion. From the time of their first employment in mills the increase has been on themselves over three hundred per cent. In Massachusetts mills women and children are from two thirds to five sixths of all employed, and the proportion in all the manufacturing portions of New England is nearly the same.

In judging the factory system as a whole, it is necessary to glance at the conditions of home work preceding it. These are given in full detail in historical and economical treatises, notably in Lecky's "History of the Eighteenth Century," and in Dr. Kay's "Moral and Physical Condition of the Working Classes." A list of the more important authorities on the subject will be found in the general bibliography at the end.

The conditions that prevailed in other countries were less strenuous with us, but the same objections to the domestic system held good at many points. In weaving, the looms occupied large part of the family living space, and overcrowding and all its evils were inevitable. Drunkenness was more common, as well as the stealing of materials by dishonest workers. Time was lost in going for material and in returning it, and only half as much was accomplished. Homes were uncared for and often filthy, and the work was done in half-lighted, airless rooms.

These conditions are often reproduced in part even to-day in buildings not adapted to their present use; but as a whole it is certain that the homes of factory-workers are cleaner, that regulation has proved beneficial, that light and air are furnished in better measure, and that overcrowding has become impossible. This applies only to textile manufactures, where machines must have room.

In an admirable chapter on the "Factory System," prepared by Colonel Carroll D. Wright for the Tenth Census of the United States, he takes up in detail the objections urged against it. These are as follows: —

> A. The factory system necessitates the employment of women and children to an injurious extent, and consequently its tendency is to destroy family life and ties and domestic habits, and ultimately the home.
>
> B. Factory employments are injurious to health.
>
> C. The factory system is productive of intemperance, unthrift, and poverty.
>
> D. It feeds prostitution, and swells the criminal list.
>
> E. It tends to intellectual degeneracy.

Under "A" there is small defence to be made. The employment of married women is fruitful of evil, and the proportion of these in Massachusetts is 23.8 per cent. Wherever this per cent is high, infant mortality is very great, being 23.5 per cent for Massachusetts and 19 per cent for Connecticut and New Hampshire. The "Labor Bureau Reports" for New Jersey treat the subject in detail, and are strongly opposed to the employment of mothers of young children outside the home; and the conclusion is the same at other points.

In the matter of general injury to health, under "B," it is stated that many factories are far better ventilated and lighted than the homes of the operatives. Ignorant employees cannot be impressed with the need of care on these points, and the air in their homes is foul and productive of disease. A cotton-mill is often better ventilated than a court-room or a lecture-room. A well-built factory allows not less than six hundred cubic feet of air space to a person, thirty to sixty cubic feet a minute being required. Ranke, in his "Elements of Physiology," makes it thirty-five a minute.

The homes of operatives have steadily improved in character; and wherever there is an intelligent class of operatives, regulations are obeyed, and sanitary conditions are fair and often perfect, while the tendency is toward more and more care in every respect. Operatives' homes are often better guarded against sanitary evils than those of farmers or the ordinary laborer.

Under "C" it is shown conclusively that the factory has diminished intemperance,—Reybaud's "History of the Factory Movement" giving full statistics on this point, as well as in regard to the growth of banks and benefit societies. The standard of living is higher here, but there are countless evidences of thrift and a general rise in condition.

In the matter of prostitution, under "D," it is shown that but eight per cent of this class come from the factory, twenty-nine per cent being from domestic service. In Lynn, Mass., a town chosen for illustration because of the large percentage of factory operatives, it was found that but seven per cent of those arrested were from this class; and this is true of all points where the foreign-born element is not largely in the majority.

Last comes the question of intellectual degeneracy, under "E." On this point it is hardly fair to make comparison of the present worker with the Lowell girl of the first period of factory labor, since she came from an educated class, and was distinctively American. Taking workers as a whole, a vast advance shows itself. Regularity and fixed rule have often been the first education in this direction; and the life, even with all its drawbacks, has the right to be regarded as an educational force, and the first step in this direction for a large proportion of the workers in it. There are points where the arraignment of Alfred, in his "History of the Factory Movement," is still true.[16] He speaks of it as a "system which jested with civilization, laughed at humanity, and made a mockery of every law of physical and moral health and of the principles of natural and social order." The "Report of the New York Bureau of Labor for 1885" shows that the charge might still be righteously brought; and Mr. Bishop gives the same testimony in his reports for New Jersey. Evil is still part of the system, and well-nigh inseparable from the methods of production and the conditions of competition; but that there are evils is recognized at all points, and thus their continuance will not and cannot be perpetuated.

FOOTNOTE:

[16] Alfred's History of the Factory Movement, vol. i. p. 27.

IV.

RISE AND GROWTH OF TRADES UP TO THE PRESENT TIME.

Defeat and discouragement attend well-nigh every step of the attempt to reach any conclusions regarding women workers in the early years of the century. It is true that 1832 witnessed an attempt at an investigation into their status, but the results were of slight value, actual figures being almost unattainable. The census of 1840 gave more, and that of 1850 showed still larger gain. In that of 1840 the number of women and children in the silk industry was taken; but while the same is true of the later one, there is apparently no record of them in any printed form. The New York State Census for the years 1845 and 1855 gave some space to the work of women and children, but there is nothing of marked value till another decade had passed.

It is to the United States Census for 1860 that we must look for the first really definite statements as to the occupations of women and children. Scattered returns of an earlier date had shown that the percentage of those employed in factories was a steadily increasing one, but in what ratio was considered as unimportant. In fact, statistics of any order had small place, nor was their need seriously felt, save here and there, in the mind of the student.

To comprehend the blankness of this period in all matters relating to social and economic questions, it is necessary to recall the fact that no such needs as those of the mother country pressed upon us. To those who looked below the surface and watched the growing tide of emigration, it was plain that they were, in no distant day, to arise; but for the most part, even for those compelled to severest toil, it was taken for granted that full support was a certainty, and that the men or women who did not earn a comfortable living could blame no one but themselves.

There were other reasons why any enumeration of women workers seemed not only superfluous but undesirable. For the better order, prejudice was still strong enough against all who deviated from custom or tradition to make each new candidate for a living shrink from any publicity that could be avoided. Society frowned upon the woman who dared to strike out in new paths, and thus made them even more thorny than necessity had already done.

It is impossible for the present, with its full freedom of opportunity, to realize, or credit even, the difficulties of the past, or even of a period hardly more than a generation ago. It was of this time that Dr. Emily Blackwell, one of the pioneers in higher work for women, wrote: —

> "Women were hindered at every turn by endless restraint in endless minor detail of habit, custom, tradition, etc.... Most women who have been engaged in any new departure would testify that the difficulties of the undertaking lay far more in these artificial hindrances and burdens than in their own health, or in the nature of the work itself."

It was this shrinking from publicity, among all save the most ordinary workers, by this time largely foreign, that made one difficulty in the way of census enumerators. By 1860 it had become plain that an enormous increase in their numbers was taking place, and that no just idea of this increase could be formed so long as industrial statistics were made up with no distinction as to sex. The spread of the factory system and the constant invention of new machinery had long ago removed from homes the few branches of the work that could be carried on within them. Processes had divided and subdivided. The mill-worker knew no longer every phase of the work implied in the production of her web, but became more and more a part of the machine itself. This was especially true of all textile industries, — cotton or woollen, with their many ramifications, — and becomes more so with each year of progress.

Cotton and woollen manufactures, with the constantly increasing subdivisions of all the processes involved, counted their thousands upon thousands of women workers. Another industry had been one of the first opened to women, much of its work being done at home. Shoemaking, with all its processes of binding and finishing, had its origin for this country in Massachusetts, to the ingenuity and enterprise of whose mechanics is due the fact that the United States has attained the highest perfection in this branch. Lynn, Mass., as far back as 1750, had become famous for its women's shoes, the making of which was carried on in the families of the manufacturers. At first no especial skill was shown; but in 1750 a Welsh shoemaker, named John Adam Dagyr, settled there and acquired great fame for himself and the town for his superior workmanship. In 1788 the exports of women's shoes from Lynn were one hundred thousand pairs, while in 1795 over three hundred thousand pairs were sent out, and by 1870 the number had reached eleven million.

Beginning with the employment of a few dozen women, twenty other towns took up the same industry, and furnish their quota of the general return. The Massachusetts Bureau of Labor gives, in its report for 1873, the number of women employed as 11,193, with some six hundred female children. Maine and New Hampshire followed, and both have a small proportion of women workers engaged in the industry, while it has gradually extended, New England always retaining the lead, till New York, Philadelphia, and many Western and Southern towns rank high in the list of producers.

As in every other trade, processes have divided and subdivided. Sewing-machines did away with the tedious binding by hand, which had its compensations, however, in the fact that it was done at home. There is only incidental record of the numbers employed in this industry till the later census returns; but the percentage outside of Massachusetts remained a very small one, as even in Maine the total number given in the Report of the Bureau of Labor for 1887 is but 533, an almost inappreciable per cent of the population. The returns of the census of 1880 give the total number of women in this employment as 21,000, the proportion still remaining largest for New England.

Straw-braiding was another of the early trades, and the first straw bonnet braided in the United States was made by Miss Betsey

Metcalf, of Providence, R.I., in 1789. For many years straw-plaiting was done at home; but the quality of our material was always inferior to that grown abroad, our climate making it much more brittle and difficult to handle. The wage at first was from two to three dollars a week; but as factories were established where imported braid was made up, the sum sometimes reached five dollars. The census of 1860 gave the total number of women employed as 1,430. According to the census of 1870, nine States had taken up this industry, Massachusetts employing the largest number, and Vermont the least, the total number being 12,594; while in 1880 the number had risen to 19,998.

Up to the time of the Civil War, aside from factory employments, the trades open to women were limited, and the majority of their occupations were still carried on at home, or with but few in numbers, as in dressmaking-establishments, millinery, and the like. With the new conditions brought about at this time, and the vast number of women thrown upon their own resources, came the flocking into trades for which there had been no training, and which had been considered as the exclusive property of men. A surplus of untrained workers at once appeared, and this and general financial depression brought the wage to its lowest terms; but when this had in part ended, the trades still remained open. At the close of the war some hundred were regarded as practicable. Ten years later the number had more than doubled, and to-day we find over four hundred occupations; while, as new inventions arise, the number of possibilities in this direction steadily increases. The many considerations involved in these facts will be met later on. General conditions of trades as a whole are given in the census returns, though even there hardly more than approximately, little work of much real value being accomplished till the formation of the labor bureaus, with which we are soon to deal. Every allowance, however, is to be made for the Census Bureau, which found itself almost incapable of overcoming many of the lions in the way. The tone of the remarks on this point in that for 1860 is almost plaintive, nor is it less so in the next; but methods have clarified, and the work is far more authoritative than for long seemed possible.

Innumerable difficulties hedged about the enumerators for 1860. Rooted objection to answering the questions in detail was not one of the least. Unfamiliarity with the newer phases of the work was another, and thus it happened that the volume when issued was full of discrepancies. The tables of occupations, for example, characterized but a little over two thousand persons as connected with woollen and worsted manufacture; while the tables of manufactures showed that considerably more than forty thousand persons were engaged, upon the average, in these branches of manufacturing industry.

The returns gave the number of women employed in various branches of manufacture as two hundred and eighty-five thousand, but stated that the figures were approximate merely, it being impossible to secure full returns. It was found that three and a half per cent of the population of Massachusetts were in the factories, and nearly the same proportion in Connecticut and Rhode Island; but details were of the most meagre description, and conclusions based upon them were likely to err at every point. Its value was chiefly educative, since the failure it represents pointed to a change in methods, and more preparation than had at any time been considered necessary in the officials who had the matter in charge.

The census for 1870 reaped the benefits of the new determination; yet even of this General Walker was forced to write: "This census concludes that from one to two hundred thousand workers are not accounted for, from the difficulty experienced in getting proper returns. The nice distinctions of foreign statisticians are impossible." And he adds: —

> "Whoever will consider the almost utter want of apprenticeship in this country, the facility with which pursuits are taken up and abandoned, and the variety and, indeed, seeming incongruity of the numerous industrial offices that are frequently united in one person, will appreciate the force of this argument.... The organization of domestic service in the United States is so crude that no distinction whatever can be successfully maintained. A census of occupations in which the attempt should be made to reach anything like European completeness in this matter would result in the return of tens of thousands of 'housekeepers' and hun-

> dreds of thousands of 'cooks,' who were simply
> 'maids of all work,' being the single servants of the
> families in which they are employed."[17]

This census gives the total number of women workers, so far as it could be determined, as 1,836,288. Of these, 191,000 were from ten to fifteen years of age; 1,594,783, from sixteen to fifty-nine; and 50,404, sixty years and over, the larger proportion of the latter division being given as engaged in agricultural employments.

In the first period of age, females pursuing gainful occupations are to males as one to three; in the second, one to six; and in the third, one to twelve. The actual increase over the numbers given in the census for 1860 is 1,551,288. The reasons for this almost incredible variation have already been suggested; and their operation became even stronger in the interval between that of 1870 and 1880. By this time methods were far more skilful and returns more minute, and thus the figures are to be accepted with more confidence than was possible with the earlier ones. The factory system, extending into almost every trade, brought about more and more differentiation of occupations, some two hundred of which were by 1880 open to women.

Comparing the rates of increase during the period between 1860 and 1870, women wage-earners had increased 19 per cent, the increase for men being but 6/97. Among the women, 6.7 per cent were engaged in agriculture, 33.4 in personal service, 7.3 in trade and transportation, and 16.5 in manufactures. In 1880 women engaged in gainful occupations formed 5.28 of the total population, and 14.68 of females over ten years of age. The present rate is not yet[18] determined; but while figures will not be accessible for some months to come, it is stated definitely that the increase will indicate nearer ten than five per cent.

The total number employed is given for this census as 2,647,157. The occupations are divided into four classes: first, agriculture; second, professional and personal services; third, trade and transportation; fourth, manufactures, mechanical and mining industries. In agriculture, 594,510 women were at work; in professional and personal services, this including domestic service, 1,361,295; trade and transportation, this including shop-girls, etc., had 59,364; while

631,988 were engaged in the last division of manufacturing, etc. Of girls from ten to fifteen years of age, agriculture had 135,862; professional and personal services, 107,830; trade, 2,547; and manufacturing, etc., 46,930. From sixteen to fifty-nine years of age there were in agriculture 435,920; in professional and personal services, 1,215,189; trade and transportation, 54,849; and manufacturing, etc., 577,157. From sixty years and upward the four classes were divided as follows: Agriculture, 22,728; professional, etc., 38,276; trade, etc., 1,968; and manufacturing, etc., 7,901.

Even for this record numbers must be added, since many women work at home and make no return of the trade they have chosen, while many others are held by pride from admitting that they work at all. But the addition of a hundred thousand for the entire country would undoubtedly cover this discrepancy in full; nor are these numbers too large, though it is impossible to more than approximate them.

Suggestive as these figures are, they are still more so when we come to their apportionment to States. They become then a history of the progress of trades, and women's share in them; and a glance enables one to determine the proportion employed in each. In the table which follows, industries are condensed under a general head, no mention being made of the many subdivisions, each ranking as a trade, but going to make up the business as a whole. It is the result of statistics taken in fifty of the principal cities, and includes only those industries in which women have the largest share.[19]

	Total Number.	Per Cent of Males	Per Cent of Females	Children
Book-binding	10,612	4,831	4,553	616
Carpet-weaving	20,371	4,960	4,207	833
Men's Clothing	160,813	4,801	5,037	159

Women's Clothing	25,192	1,030	8,833	137
Cotton Goods	185,472	3,457	4,914	1,629
Men's Furnishing Goods	11,174	1,140	8,560	300
Hosiery and Knitting	28,885	2,602	6,130	1,268
Millinery and Lace	25,687	1,120	8,637	243
Shirts	6,555	1,481	8,000	513
Silk and Silk Goods	31,337	2,992	5,232	1,776
Straw Goods	10,948	2,991	6,850	154
Tobacco	32,756	4,544	3,290	2,166
Umbrellas and Canes	3,608	4,169	5,152	679
Woollen Goods	86,504	54,544	3,395	1,174
Worsted Goods	18,800	5,431	5,038	1,540

In obtaining these averages, it was found necessary to equalize the returns of Pittsburg and Philadelphia, the former having but 4.55 per cent of women workers, while Philadelphia had 31. This resulted from the fact that the industries of Philadelphia are the manufacturing of textiles and other goods, which employ women chiefly; while Pittsburg has principally iron and steel mills. New York was found to have 31 per cent of women workers; Lowell, Mass., had 47.42, and Manchester, N.H., 53; Pittsburg and Wilmington, Del., having the lowest percentage.

The gain of women in trades over the census of 1870 was sixty-four per cent, the total percentage of women workers for the whole country being forty-nine. The ten years just ended show a still larger percentage; and many of the trades which a decade since still hesitated to admit women, are now open, those regarded as most peculiarly the province of men having received many feminine recruits. These isolated or scattered instances hardly belong here, and are mentioned simply as indications of the general trend. Wise or unwise, experiment is the order of the day, its principal service in many cases being to test untried powers, and break down barriers, built up often by mere tradition, and not again to rise till women themselves decide when and where.

Taking States in their alphabetical order, the census of 1880 gives the number of working-women for each as follows:[20] —

Alabama, 124,056.

Arizona, 471.

Arkansas, 30,616.

California, 28,200.

Colorado, 4,779.

Connecticut, 48,670.

Dakota, 2,851.

Delaware, 7,928.

District of Columbia, 19,658.

Florida, 17,781.

Georgia, 152,322.

Idaho, 291.

Illinois, 106,101.

Missouri, 62,943.

Montana, 507.

Nebraska, 10,455.

Nevada, 403.

New Hampshire, 30,128.

New Jersey, 66,776.

New Mexico, 2,262.

New York, 360,381.

North Carolina, 86,976.

Ohio, 112,639.

Oregon, 2,779.

Pennsylvania, 216,980.

Rhode Island, 29,859.

Indiana, 51,422.

Iowa, 44,845.

Kansas, 54,422.

Louisiana, 95,052.

Maine, 33,528.

Massachusetts, 174,183.

Michigan, 55,013.

Minnesota, 25,077.

Mississippi, 110,416.

South Carolina, 120,087.

Tennessee, 56,408.

Texas, 58,943.

Utah, 2,877.

Vermont, 16,167.

Washington Territory, 1,060.

West Virginia, 11,508.

Wisconsin, 46,395.

Wyoming, 464.

FOOTNOTES:

[17] Remarks on Tables of Occupations, Ninth Census of the United States, Population and Social Statistics, p. 663.

[18] June, 1893.

[19] The table is copied with minute care from that given in the last census; and while it shows one or two deficiencies, the writer is in no sense responsible for them, its accuracy, as a whole, not being affected by the slight discrepancy referred to.

[20] The tables in this department of the census for 1890 are not yet ready for the public; but the department states that the increase in women wage-earners averages about ten per cent.

V.

LABOR BUREAUS AND THEIR WORK IN RELATION TO WOMEN.

The difficulties encountered by the enumerators of the United States Census, and the growing conviction that much more minute and organized effort must be given if the real status of women workers was to be obtained, had already been matter of grave discussion. The labor question pressed upon all who looked below the surface of affairs; and very shortly after the census of 1860 a proposition was made in Boston to establish there a formal bureau of labor, whose business should be to fill in all the blanks that in the general work were passed over.

Many facts, all pointing to the necessity of some such organization, lay before the men who pondered the matter, — factory abuses of many orders, the startling increase of pauperism and crime, with other causes which can find small space here. With difficulty consent was obtained to establish a bureau which should inquire into the causes of all this; and the first report was given to the public in 1870. It was descriptive rather than statistical, and necessarily so. Methods were still a matter of question and experiment. The public had small interest in the project, and it was essential to outline, not only the work to be done, but the reasons for its need.

Naturally, then, the volume touched upon many abuses,— children in factories, and the factory system as a whole; the homes of workers, and their needs in sanitary and other directions; and toward the end a few pages of special comment on the hard lives of working-women as a whole.

The report for 1871 followed the same lines, giving more detail to each. That for 1872 took up various phases of women's work,[21] with some of the general conditions then existing. For the following year elaborate tables of the cost of living were given, and are invaluable as matters of reference; and in 1874 came a no less important contribution to social science in the report on the "Homes of Working-People." Those of working-women were of course included, but there was still no description of many of the conditions known to hedge them about. Each inquiry, however, turned attention more and more in this direction, and emphasized the need of some work given exclusively to women workers.

In 1875 attention was directed to the health of working-women, and a portion of the report was devoted to the special effects of certain forms of employment upon the health of women,[22] the education of children, the conditions of families, etc. That for 1876 discussed the question of wives' earnings, and gave tables of what proportion they made; and that for 1877 took up "Pauperism and Crime," in the growing amount of which it was claimed by many that the worker had large share.

In 1878 large space was given to education and the work of the young, for whom the half-time system was urged. The conjugal condition of wives and mothers was also considered, and the bearing of their work upon the home. The financial distress of the period had affected wages, and the report for 1879 considered the effect of this, with the condition of the "unemployed," the tramp question, and other phases of the problem. With 1880 and the ending of the first decade of work in this direction came a fuller report on the social life of workingmen and the divorces in Massachusetts; 1881 made a plea for uniform hours, and 1882 was devoted to wages, prices, and profits, and further details of the life of operatives within their homes; and 1883 found reason again to go over the question of wages and prices.

I have given this detail because, when one views the work of the bureau as a whole, it will be seen that each year formed one step toward the final result, which has been of most vital bearing upon all since accomplished in the same direction for women. Until the appearance of the report for 1884, on the "Working-Girls of Boston," there had been no absolute and authoritative knowledge as to their lives, their earnings, and their status as a whole. Their numbers were equally unknown, nor was there interest in their condition, save here and there among special students of social science. On the other hand there was a popular impression that the ranks of prostitution were recruited from the manufactory, and that a certain stigma necessarily rested upon the factory-worker and indeed upon working-girls as a class.

Six divisions had been found essential to the thorough handling of the subject; and these divisions have formed the basis of all work since done in the same lines, whether in State bureaus or in that of the United States, soon to find mention here. It was under the direction of Colonel Carroll D. Wright that the Massachusetts Bureau did its careful and scientific work; and he represents the most valuable labor in this direction that the country has had, deserving to rank in this matter, as Tench Coxe still does in the manufacturing system, as the "Father" of the labor-bureau system.

The six divisions settled upon as essential to any general system of reports were as follows: —

       1. Social Condition.
       2. Occupations, Places in which Employed.
       3. Hours of Labor, Time Lost, etc.
       4. Physical and Sanitary Condition.
       5. Economic Condition.
       6. Moral Condition.

The Tenth Census of the United States gave the number of women employed in the city of Boston as 38,881, 20,000 of whom were in occupations other than domestic service. Each year, as we have already seen, had touched more and more nearly upon the facts bound up in their lives, but it had become necessary to determine with an accuracy that could not be brought in question precisely the facts given under the six headings. To the surprise of the special agents detailed for this work, who had anticipated disagreeables of every order, the girls themselves took the liveliest interest in the matter, answered questions freely, and gave every facility for the fullest searching into each phase involved. American girls were found to form but 22.3 per cent of the whole number of working-women in Massachusetts, of whom but 58.4 per cent had been born in that State.

The results reached in this report may be regarded as a summary, not only of conditions for Boston, but for all the large manufacturing towns of New England, later inquiry justifying this conclusion.

The average age of working-girls was found to be 24.81 years, and the average at which they began work, 16.81; the average time actually at work, 7.49 years, and the average number of occupations followed 178, the time spent in each being 4.43 years. Of the whole, 85 per cent were found to do their own housework and sewing, either wholly or in part.

But 22 per cent were allowed any vacation, and but 3.9 per cent received pay during that time, the average vacation being 1.87 weeks. A little over 26 per cent worked the full year without loss of time, while an average of 12.32 weeks was lost by 73 per cent. The average time worked by all during the year was 42.95 weeks. In personal service 26.5 per cent worked more than ten hours a day; in trade, 19.5 per cent were so employed, and in manufactures 5.6 per cent. In all occupations 8.9 per cent worked more than ten hours a day, and 8.6 per cent more than sixty hours a week.

In the matter of health 76.2 per cent of the whole number employed were in good health.

The average weekly earnings for the average time employed, 42.95 weeks, was $6.01, and the average weekly earnings of all the working-girls of Boston for a whole year were $4.91. The average weekly income, including earnings, assistance, and income from extra work done by many, was $5.17 a year.

The average yearly income from all sources was $269.70, and the average yearly expenses for positive needs $261.30, leaving but

$7.77, on the average, as a margin for books, amusements, etc. Those making savings are 11 per cent of the whole, their average savings being $72.15 per year. A few run in debt, the average debt being $36.60 for the less than 3 per cent incurring debt.

Of the total average yearly expenses, these percentages being based upon the law laid down by Dr. Engels of Prussia, as to percentage of expenses belonging to subsistence, 63 per cent must be expended for food and lodging, and 25 per cent for clothing,—a total of 88 per cent of total expenses for subsistence and clothing, leaving but 12 per cent of total expense to be distributed to the other needs of living.

These are, briefly summed up, the results of the investigation, in which the single workers constituted 88.9 of the whole, and the married but 6 per cent, widows making up the number. It is impossible in these limits to give further detail on these points, all readers being referred to the report itself.

The same questions that had first sought answer in New England were even more pressing in New York. As in most subjects of deep popular or scientific importance, the sense of need for more data by which to judge seemed in the air; and already the Labor Bureau of the State of New York, under the efficient guidance of Mr. Charles F. Peck, had begun a course of inquiries of the same nature. For years, beginning with the New York "Tribune," in the days when Margaret Fuller worked for it and touched at times upon social questions,—always in the mind of Horace Greeley, its founder,— there had been periodical stirs of feeling in behalf of sewing-women. It was known that the enormous influx of foreign labor naturally massed at this point, more than could ever be possible elsewhere, had brought with it evils suspected, but still not yet defined in any sense to be trusted. Indications on the surface were seriously bad, but actual investigation had never tested their nature or degree. The report of the bureau for 1885, which was given to the public in 1886, met with a degree of interest and study not usually accorded these volumes, and roused public feeling to an unexpected extent.

Mr. Peck brought to the work much the same order of interest that had marked that of Colonel Wright, and wrote in his introduction to the report the summary of the situation for New York City: —

> "By reason of its immense population, its numerous and extensive manufactures, its wealth, its poverty, and general cosmopolitan character, New York City presents a field for investigation into the subject of 'Working-Women, their Trades, Wages, Home and Social Conditions,' unequalled by any other centre of population in America. It opens up a wider and more diversified field for inquiry, study, and classification of the various industries in which women seek employment, than can be found even in European cities, with but few if any exceptions. It is for such reasons that the inquiry of the bureau into this special subject has been largely confined to the city named."

Two hundred and forty-seven trades are given in this report, in which some two hundred thousand women were found to be engaged, this being exclusive of domestic service. The divisions of the subject were substantially those adopted by the Massachusetts Bureau; but the numbers and complexity of conditions made the inquiry far more difficult. Its results and their bearings will find place later on. It is sufficient now to say that the two may be regarded as summarizing all phases of work for women, and as an index to the difficulties at all other points in the country.

The Bureau of Labor for Connecticut sent out its first report in the same year (1885), and included investigations and statistics in the same lines, though, for reasons specified, in much more limited degree. That for 1886 for the same State took up in detail some points in regard to the work of both women and children, which, for want of both time and space, had been omitted in the first, their returns coinciding in all important particulars with those of the other bureaus.

In 1886 the California Bureau of Labor touched the same points, but only incidentally, in its general analysis of the labor question. In the following year, however, the report covering the years 1887 and 1888 took up the question under the same aspects as those handled in the special reports on this topic, and gave full treatment of the wages, lives, and general conditions for working-women. It included, also, the facts, so far as they could be ascertained, of the nature, wages, and conditions of domestic service in California,—the first attempt at treating this difficult subject with any accuracy. The apprentice system, and an important chapter on manual training and its bearings make this report one of the most valuable, from the social point of view, that has been given, though where all are invaluable it is hard to characterize one above another.

Mr. Tobin, for California, and Mr. Hutchins, for Iowa, seemed moved at the same time in much the same way,—the Iowa report for 1887 treating the many questions involved with that largeness which has thus far distinguished work in this direction. Kansas, in the report for 1888, gave general conditions, women being treated incidentally; and Minnesota, in the report for the years 1887 and 1888, gave a chapter on working-women, wages, etc.

Colorado followed, giving in the report for 1887 and 1888, under the management of Commissioner Rice, a chapter on women wage-workers, in which space is given to certified complaints of the women themselves, as to what they consider the disabilities of their special trades. Domestic service, with some of its abuses, was also considered, and is of much value. These reports sum up the work so far done in the West, where labor bureaus are of recent growth. The spirit of inquiry is, however, equally alive; and each year will see minuter detail and a deeper scientific spirit.

Maine, in the report for 1888, took up many questions of general interest, with their incidental bearings on the work of women; and in 1889 came another report from Kansas, in which the labor commissioner, Mr. Frank Betton, gave large space to an investigation conducted under many difficulties, but covering the ground very fully. A very full report from Michigan, under Commissioner Henry A. Robinson, was issued in 1892, nearly two hundred pages being given to an exhaustive examination into the conditions of women wage-earners in the State, its methods owing much to the work which had preceded it.

With this background of admirable work always, no matter what might be the limitations, making each report a little broader in purpose and minuter in detail, the way was plain for something even more comprehensive. This was furnished by the Bureau of Labor of the United States, which had changed its name, and become, in June, 1887, the Department of Labor, a part of the Department of the Interior. This report—the fourth from the bureau, and issued in 1888—was entitled "Working-Women in Large Cities," and included investigations made in twenty-two cities, from Boston to San Francisco and San José.

All that long experience had demonstrated as most important in such work was brought to bear. The investigation covered manual labor in cities, excluding textile industries, save incidentally as these had already been treated, as well as domestic service. Textile factories are usually outside of large cities, and it was the object to discover the opportunities of employment in the way of manual labor in cities themselves.

Three hundred and forty-three distinct industries showed themselves, and others were found which were not included, it being safe to say that some four hundred may be considered open to women. As before stated, many are simply subdivisions, made by the constantly increasing complexity of machinery. The agents of the department carried their work into the lowest and worst places in the cities named, because in such places are to be found women who are struggling for a livelihood in most respectable callings,— living in them as a matter of necessity, since they cannot afford to live otherwise, but leaving them whenever wages are sufficient to admit of change.

It is this report which forms the summary of all the work that has preceded it, and that gives the truest exponent of all present conditions. It is only necessary to add to it the summaries of the State reports at other points, to see the aspect of the question as a whole; and thus we are ready to consider by its aid the general rates of wages and of the status of the trades of every nature in which women are now engaged.

FOOTNOTES:

[21] Report for 1872, pp. 59-108.

[22] Report for 1875, pp. 67-112.

VI.

PRESENT WAGE-RATES IN THE UNITED STATES.

Under this heading it is proposed to include, not only the trades just specified as coming under the investigations recorded in "Working-Women in Large Cities," but also such data as can be gleaned from all the labor reports which have given any attention to this phase of the labor question. Naturally, then, we turn to the report of the Massachusetts Bureau for 1881, the first statement of these points, and compare it with the results obtained in the last report from Washington, as well as with the returns from the various States where investigation of the question has been made.

Exceptionally favorable conditions would seem to belong to the year in which the report for 1884 appeared. The financial distress of 1877, with its results, had passed. New industries of many orders had opened up for women, and trade in all its forms called for workers and gave almost constant employ, save in the few occupations which have a distinct season, and oblige those engaged in them to divide their time between two if a living is assured.

A distinction must at once be made in the definition of earnings. In speaking of them, there are necessarily three designations,— wages, earnings, and income. Wages represent the actual pay per week at the time employed, with no reference to the number of weeks' employment during the year. Earnings are the total receipts for any year from wages. Thus, for example, a girl is paid $5 a week wages, and works forty weeks of her year. Her earnings would then be for the year $200, though her wages of $5 per week would indicate that she earned $260 a year; while in fact her average weekly earnings would be for the whole year $3.84. Income is her total receipts for the year from all sources: wages, extra work, help from friends or from investments; in fact, any receipts from which expenses can be paid.

In preparing the tables of these reports, the highest, the lowest, the average, and the general average were brought into a final comparison. Often but one wage is given, and it then becomes naturally both highest and lowest; but all figures are made to indicate an entire occupation or branch of industry, and not a few high or low paid employees in that branch. It is only with the final comparison that we are able to deal, the reader being referred to the reports themselves for the invaluable details given at full length and including many hundred pages.

The divisions of occupations are the same as those of the tenth census, and the tables are made on the same system. To determine the general conditions for the twenty thousand at work, it was necessary to have accurate detail as to one thousand; and, in fact, 1,032 were interviewed. Directly after the work in this direction had ended, and before the report was ready for publication, a general reduction of ten per cent in wages took place, and this must be kept in mind in dealing with the returns recorded. In this, recapitulation is given in full, and, as will be seen, includes all occupations open to women.

RECAPITULATION

	BOSTON.		OTHER PARTS OF MASS.		OTHER STATES.	
	Number.	Average weekly earnings.	Number.	Average weekly earnings.	Number.	Average weekly earnings.
Government and professional	7	$5 57	5	$6 40	10	$6 28
Domestic and personal office	178	5 94	27	5 33	21	4 69
Trade and transportation	221	5 00	4	9 25	4	7 25
Manufactures and mechanical industries	1,293	6 22	72	7 06	49	7 58
All occupations	1,699	$6 03	108	$6 68	84	$6 69

The commissioners of the New York State Bureau of Labor followed a slightly different method. The returns are no less minute, but are given under the heading of each trade, two hundred and forty-seven of which were investigated. The wages of workwomen for the entire year run from $3.50 to $4 a week, the general average not being given, though later returns make it $5.85. This is, however, for skilled labor; and as a vast proportion of women workers in New York City are engaged in sewing, the poorest paid of all industries, we must accept the first figures as nearer the truth. An expert on shirts receives as high as $12 a week, in some cases $15; but in slop work, and under the sweating-system, wages fall to $2.50 or $3 per week, and at times less. Mr. Peck found cloakmakers working on the most expensive and perfectly finished garments for 40 cents a day, a full day's pay being from 50 to 60 cents.[23] In other cases a day's work brought in but 25 cents, and seventeen overalls of blue denim gave a return of 75 cents. Two and a half cents each is paid for the making of boys' gingham waists, with trimming on neck and sleeves, including the button-holes; and the women who made these sat sixteen hours at the sewing-machine, with a result of 25 cents.[24]

This was for irregular work. Women employed on clothing in general, working for reputable firms, receive from $4.50 to $6 per week. In the tobacco manufacture, in which great numbers are employed, $9 is the lowest actual earnings, and $20 the highest per week. In cigarettes, the pay ranges from $4 to $15 per week. In dry-goods, with ten divisions of employment,—cashiers, bundle-girls, saleswomen, floor-walkers, seamstresses, cloakmakers, cash-girls, stock-girls, milliners, and sewing-girls,—the lowest sum per week is $1.50, paid to cash-girls, and the highest paid to floor-walkers, $16. On the east side of the city, shop girls receive often as low as $3 per week; in a few cases specified, $2.50 per week.[25]

In laundry-work, which includes several divisions, wages weekly range from $7.50 to $10, though ironers of special excellence sometimes make from $12 to $15 per week. In millinery the wages are from $6 to $7 per week. In preserving and fruit-canning wages are from $3.50 to $10, the average worker earning about $5 per week. Mr. Peck states that in fashion trades the two distinct seasons bring the year's earnings to about six months. "Learners" in the trades coming under this head receive $1.50 per week. Saleswomen suffer also from season trade, as it necessitates reduction of force. The better class of workers receive from $8 to $15 per week, while heads of departments range from $25 to $50, or even higher, for exceptional merit. These cases are of the rarest, however, the wage as an average falling below that of Boston.

But three State reports cover the same dates as these already quoted (1885 and 1886),—Connecticut, New Jersey, and California, the former being for 1885. In this, women's wages are given incidentally in general tables, and must be disentangled to find any average. In artificial flowers the highest wage is given as $7, and the lowest $3, the average being $5. In blankets and woollen goods the highest is $12.50 and the lowest $6, an average of $9 per week. In factory work of all orders, wages range from $6 to $9.75 per week, the average paid to women and girls being $7.50 per week. In clothing, including underwear, wages are from $3 to $15 per week, and the average annual income of women in these trades is given as $300 per year. In cloakmaking the lowest wage is $3, the highest $9, and the average $7.50. The average wage for San Francisco is given as $6.95, and that for the whole State is about $6. The Connecticut report for 1885 gives simply the yearly wage in various trades. Reason for this is found in the fact that it was the first, and could thus deal with the subject only tentatively. Clothing is given as producing for women a yearly average of $229, and shirts $237. Factory work gave $207, paper boxes $227, and woollen goods $245.

In the report for 1886, the lowest average wage is reported as found in the making of wearing apparel; but the average for the State was found to be a trifle over $6.50 per week.

The report from New Jersey makes the lowest wages $3 per week, and the highest $10, the average being $5. This report covers ground more fully and in more varied directions than any one of the same period, though there is only incidental reference to the work of women as a whole, the returns being given in the general tables of wages. Wages and the cost of living are compared, and the chapter under this head is one of the most valuable in the summary of reports as a whole. The report for 1886 gives the same general average of wages for the State, but adds an exhaustive treatment of "Earnings, Cost of Living, and Prices."

Maine sent out its first annual report in 1887, and gives the wages of women workers as $3.58 for the lowest, and $15.20 for the highest, the annual earnings ranging from $104 to $520. The report from the same State for 1889 takes up the subject of working-women in detail, giving their home or boarding conditions, sanitary conditions, their own remarks on trades, wages, etc., and the aspect of their labor as a whole. The average wage remains the same.

Rhode Island, in its Third Annual Report for 1889, under the direction of Commissioner Almon K. Goodwin, gives the average wage for the State as $5.87, and devotes the bulk of its space to working-women, with full returns from the entire State.

For the same year California, by its labor commissioner, Mr. John J. Tobin, gives an equally exhaustive statement of the conditions of women wage-earners in that State. The lowest weekly wage given is $5, and the highest $11. Plain cooks receive from $25 to $40 a month with board and lodging, and domestic servants from $15 to $25 with board. In cloak-making the lowest wage is $3, and the highest $7.50; and in shirt-making the lowest is $2.50, and the highest $6. General clothing and underwear range from $4.50 to $6, and other trades average a trifle higher wage than in New England. The chapter on domestic service is suggestive and important, and the whole treatment makes the report a necessity to all who would understand the situation in detail. This, however, is so true of all that have touched upon the subject that it appears invidious to single out any one alone. They must be taken together. With each year the scientific value of each increases, and there appears to be distinct emulation among the commissioners as to which shall embody the most in the returns made and the general treatment of the whole.

The first report from Colorado, issued in 1888, Mr. James Rice commissioner, devotes a chapter to women wage-earners, with an additional one on domestic service and its drawbacks. The average wage for the State is given as $6; and the commissioner states that notwithstanding the general impression that higher wages are paid in Colorado than at any other point save California, actual returns show that the average sums in several occupations are less than that paid to persons similarly employed in cities along the Atlantic seaboard.

Kansas, in its fifth annual report issued in 1889, gives a section to working-women. The commissioner, Mr. Frank Betton, considers the returns imperfect, great difficulty having been experienced in securing them. The average weekly wage is given as $5.17. Expenses are carefully analyzed, and there is a report of the remarks of employers, as well as from a number of those employed.

In the report from Iowa for 1887, Commissioner Hutchins laments that so few women have been willing to fill out blanks of returns. The wage returns given range from $3.75 to $9. The report for 1889 makes mention of continued difficulties in securing returns, and gives the annual earnings of women as from \$100 to \$440. The tables include cost of living and many other essential particulars.

Wisconsin, in the report for 1884, has a chapter on working-girls. It gives the average weekly income in personal services as \$5.25; in trade, \$4.18; in manufactures, \$5.22, and the general average for the year as \$5.17.

Minnesota, whose first report, under the supervision of Commissioner John Lamb, appeared in 1888 for the years 1887 and 1888, found little or no room for statistics, but included a chapter on working-women, with a few admirable tables of age, nativity, home and working conditions, etc. Minute inquiry was made as to cost of living, clothing, etc.; and the results form a chapter of painful interest, that on domestic service being equally suggestive. Clothing, as usual, represents the lowest average wage, \$3.66 per week, the highest being \$8.50, and the general average a trifle over \$6.

Michigan, in 1890, under its labor commissioner, Mr. Henry A. Robinson, added to the list one of the most thorough studies yet made of general conditions. The agents of the bureau, trained for the work, made personal visits to working-women and girls to the number of 13,436, this representing one hundred and thirty-seven distinct industries and three hundred and seventy-eight occupations. The blanks prepared for filling out contained one hundred and twenty-nine questions, classified as follows: Social, 28; industrial, 12; hours of labor, 14; economic, 54; sanitary, 21, with seven others as to dress, societies, church attendance, with remarks and suggestions from the workers themselves. As usual, in such cases, employers here and there objected to any investigation, fearing labor organizations were at the bottom of it; but the majority allowed free examination. The report is very full, and gives a clear and full view of the individual lives of this body of women workers. The average wage proved to be \$4.81 per week, the average income for the year being \$216.45. The average income of teachers and those in public positions was \$457.27.

This is the showing, State by State, so far as bureaus have reported. Many States have made no move in this direction; but interest is now thoroughly aroused, and the subject is likely to find treatment in all, this depending somewhat, however, on the character of the State industries and the numbers at work in each. Manufacturing necessarily brings with it conditions that in the end compel inquiry; and for most of the Southern States such industries are still new, while the West has not yet found the same occasion as the East for full knowledge of the problems involved in woman's work and wages.

We come now to the most elaborate and far-reaching inquiry yet made, — the work of the United States Bureau of Labor under Commissioner Wright, entitled "Working-Women in Large Cities." Twenty-two of these are reported upon after one of the most rigorous examinations ever undertaken; and the average wage of each tallies with the rates given in the States to which they belong. Taken alphabetically, the list is as follows: —

AVERAGE WEEKLY EARNINGS, BY CITIES.

Atlanta	$4.95	New Orleans	$4.31
Baltimore	4.18	New York	5.85
Boston	5.64	Philadelphia	5.34
Brooklyn	5.76	Providence	5.51
Buffalo	4.27	Richmond	3.83
Charleston, S.C.	4.22	St. Louis	5.19
Chicago	5.74	St. Paul	6.62
Cincinnati	4.50	San Francisco	6.91
Cleveland	4.63	San José	6.11
Indianapolis	4.57	Savannah	4.90
Louisville	4.51		----
Newark	5.20	All Cities	5.24

In addition to these figures, it seems well to give the average yearly earnings of women in some of the most profitable industries, those being chosen which are seldom affected by "seasons": —

Artificial flowers, $277.53; awnings and tents, $276.46; bookbinding, $271.31; boots and shoes, $286.60; candy, $213.59; carpets, $298.53; cigar boxes, $267.36; cigar factory, $294.66; cigarette factory, $266.12; cloak factory, $291.76; clothing factory, $248.36; cotton-mills, $228.32; dressmaking, $278.37; dry-goods stores, $368.84; jewelry factory, $263.80; men's furnishing-goods factory, $232.24; millinery, $345.95; paper-box factory, $240.47; plug-tobacco factory, $235.67; printing-office, $300; skirt factory, $265.40; smoking-tobacco factory, $238.70.

These, so far as they have been collected and tabulated by the various labor bureaus, are the returns for the United States as a whole. The reports for the following years of 1891 and 1892 were expected to be far more general, but this has not proved to be the case.

AVERAGE WAGE PER STATE.

Maine	$5.50
Massachusetts	6.68
Connecticut	6.50
Rhode Island	5.87
New York	5.85
New Jersey	5.00
California	6.00
Colorado	6.00
Kansas	5.17
Wisconsin	5.17
Minnesota	6.00
All cities	5.24

FOOTNOTES:

[23] Third Annual Report of New York Bureau of Labor, p. 162. These are Mr. Peck's figures; but the United States report gives the average for skilled labor as $5.85 per week, and adds that the unskilled earns far less.

[24] Ibid. p. 165.

[25] New York Bureau of Statistics of Labor, Third Annual Report, p. 27.

VII.

GENERAL CONDITIONS FOR ENGLISH WORKERS.

So far as opportunity is concerned, it is the United States only that offers a practically unlimited field to women workers, to whom some four hundred trades and occupations are now open. Comparison with other countries is, however, essential, if we would judge fairly of conditions as a whole; and thus we turn first to that other English-speaking race, and the English worker at home. At once we are faced with the impossibility of gathering much more than surface indications, since in no other country is there any counterpart to our admirable system of investigation and tabulation, each year more and more systematic and thorough. In spite of the fact that factory laws had their birth in England, and that the whole system of child labor—the early horrors of which find record in thousands of pages of special reports from inspectors appointed by government—has been through their means modified and improved, there are, even now, no sources of information as to numbers at work or the characteristics of special industries. The census must be the chief dependence; and here we find the enormous proportions to which the employment of women has attained.

In 1861 these returns gave for England and Wales 1,024,277 women at work. Twenty years later the number had doubled, half a million being found in London alone. This does not include all, since, as Mr. Charles Booth notes in his recent "Labor and Life of the People," many employed women do not return their employments.

Mr. Booth's work is a purely private enterprise, assisted by devoted co-workers, and by trained experts employed at his own expense. For the final estimate must be added general census returns, and the recent reports on the sweating-system in London and other English cities.

Beginning with factory operatives and their interests, nothing is easier than to follow the course of legislation on their behalf. The "Life of Lord Shaftesbury" is, in itself, the history of the movement for the protection of women and children,—a movement begun early in the present century, and made imperative by the hideous disclosures of oppression and outrage, not only among factory operatives, but the women and children in mining and other industries. Active as were his efforts and those of his colleagues, it is only within a generation that the fruit of their labor is plainly seen. As late as 1844, at the time Engel's notable book on "The Condition of the Working-Class in England" appeared, the labor of children of four and five years was still permitted; and women and children alike worked in mines, in brickyards, and other exposed and dangerous employments for the merest pittance. The pages of Engel's book swarm with incidents of individual and class misery; and while he admits fully, in the appendix prepared in 1886, that many of the evils enumerated have disappeared, he adds that for the mass of workers "the state of misery and insecurity in which they live now is as low as ever, perhaps lower."

Year by year, in spite of constant agitation and the unceasing effort of Lord Shaftesbury to alter the worst abuses, these evils remained, and faced the examiner into social problems, slight ameliorations here and there serving chiefly to throw into darker relief the misery of the situation. Not only the philanthropist but officials joined hands; and in the proceedings of the British Association for the Advancement of Science, each year added to the number and importance of the protests against an iniquitous system.

Chief among these protests ranked that against the overwork of pregnant mothers, through which, as one of the most able opponents of existing evils, W. Stanley Jevons, wrote, "infinite, irreparable wrong is done to helpless children," adding that the appalling infant mortality of the manufacturing districts attracted far less attention and interest in the public mind than the death of a single murderer. At nearly the same time Mr. F.W. Lowndes gave the fruit of long research in a paper read before the British Association for the Advancement of Science, entitled "The Destruction of Infancy;"[26] and this was supplemented by testimony from experts, the Statistical Society adding weighty testimony to the same effect.[27]

From these and other official testimony it was found that in nineteen manufacturing towns,[28] out of 1,023,896 children [Forty-first Report of the Registrar-General, p. 36] born, 82,259 died in infancy. The rate of mortality varied from 59.4 in Portsmouth through an ascending scale, being in London 78.6 and in Liverpool the almost incredible proportion of 103.6 per thousand. In a rural country infant mortality does not exceed from thirty-five to forty per thousand. The Report of the Select Committee on the Protection of Infant Life was filled with details so horrible that only the sworn testimony of experts made them credited at all.[29]

Dr. Hunter's report on rural mortality shows that when mothers are employed in what are known as "field gangs" for out-of-door work, leaving their children in the charge of old women too weak for such labor as their own, that infants died like sheep. Godfrey's Cordial was the chief engine of destruction; the corps of inspectors who reported to the Government finding infants in all stages of prostration, from the overdoses of the popular specific warranted to render any attention from nurse or mother quite unnecessary.

As to the direct effects of factory or out-door labor on pregnant mothers, out of 10,000 births among factory mothers, there died from 1863-75 of children under one year of age, in Portsmouth 1,459, Liverpool 2,189, London 1,591, and other towns with textile industries 1,940. Statistics taken in Germany and at other points all went to show that in the matter of out-door labor at the harvest season, when all women-workers are in the fields, the deaths of nursing infants were three times as great as in the other nine months.

For details and deduction from these facts the reader is referred to the reports themselves. "I go so far," wrote Mr. Jevons, "as to advocate the ultimate complete exclusion of mothers of children under the age of three years from factories and workshops;" and his conviction voiced that of every examiner into the situation as it stood at that time.

The Factory and Workshop Act came as partial solution to the many problems; and though regarded by the working-class as a mass of arbitrary restrictions whose usefulness they denied and in whose benefits they had no faith, it has actually proved the Great Charter of the working-classes. There are points still to be altered, — modifications made necessary by the constant change in methods of production, as well as in the enlarging sense of the ethical principles involved. But our own legislation is still far behind it at many points, and its work is done efficiently and thoroughly. Laws had been made, one by one, fifteen standing on the Statute Books in 1878, when all were abrogated, their essential features being codified in the Act as it stands to-day, — a genuine industrial code in one hundred and seven sections.

Up to this date violation of its provisions had been incessant; but determined enforcement brought about a uniform working day, protection of dangerous machinery, proper ventilation, improved sanitary conditions, an interdict on Sunday labor, and many other reforms in administration. Fourteen years have seen next to no change in the Act, and the condition of women and child workers in factories and workshops has come to be regarded as the best that modern systems of production admit. These workers, whose numbers now mount to hundreds of thousands, are a class apart, and for them legislation has accomplished all that legislation seems able to do in alleviating social miseries. Content with the results achieved, need of further effort in other directions failed of recognition, and apathy became the general condition.

It was during this season of repose that the public mind received first one shock and then another. "The Bitter Cry of Outcast London" appalled all who read; and leaf by leaf the new book of revelations disclosed always deeper depths of misery and want among all workers with the needle,—from the days of the fig-leaf the symbol of grinding toil and often hopeless misery.

Not alone from professional agitators, so called, but from philanthropists of every order, came the cry for help. The Factory and Workshop Act had not touched home labor. The sweating-system, born of modern conditions, had risen unsuspected, and ran riot, not only in East London, but even in back alleys of the sacred west, and in the swarming southwest region beyond London Bridge. The London "Lancet," the most authoritative medical journal of the world, conservative as it has always been, has at last found that it must join hands with socialist and anarchist, "scientific" or otherwise, with philanthropists of every order, against the new evil and its horrors. Rich and poor alike were involved. The virus of the deadly conditions under which the garments took shape was implanted in every stitch that held them together, and transferred itself to the wearer. Not only from London, but from every city of England, came the same cry; and the public faced suddenly an abyss of misery whose existence had been unknown and unsuspected, and the causes of which seemed inexplicable.

For many months of the year just ended (1892) parliamentary investigation has gone on. Report after report has been made to its committees; and as testimony from accredited sources poured in, incidentally a flood of light has been let in upon many forms of work outside the clothing-manufacturer. To-day, in four huge volumes of some thousand pages each, one may read the testimony, heart-sickening in every detail,—a noted French political economist, the Comte d'Haussonville, describing it, in a recent article in "La Revue des deux Mondes" as "The Martyrology of English Industries."

In such conditions inspection is inoperative. An army of inspectors would not suffice where every house represents from one to a dozen workshops under its roof, in each of which sanitary conditions are defied, and the working day made more often fourteen and sixteen hours than twelve. Even for this day a starvation wage is the rule; the sewing-machine operative, for example, while earning a wage of fifteen or eighteen pence, furnishing her own thread and being forced to pay rental on the machine.

A portion of a wage table is given here as illustrative of rates, and used as a reference table before the preparation of Mr. Booth's book, which gives much the same figures: —

> Making paper bags, 41/2d. to 51/2d. per thousand; possible earnings, 5s. to 6s. per week.

> Button-holes, 3d. a dozen; possible earnings, 8s. a week.

> Shirts, 2d. each, worker finding her own cotton; can get six done between 8 A.M. and 11 P.M.

> Sack sewing, 6d. for twenty-five; 8d. to 1s. 6d. per hundred. Possible earnings, 8s. per week.

> Pill-box making, 9s. for thirty-six gross; possible earnings, 8s. per week.

> Shirt button-hole making, 1d. a dozen; can do three or four dozen a day.

> Whip-making, 1s. a dozen; can do a dozen a day.

> Trousers finishing, 3d. to 5d. each, finding one's own cotton; can do four a day.

> Shirt-finishing, 3d. to 4d. a dozen; possible earnings, 6s. a week.

Outside of the cities, where the needle is almost the sole refuge of the unskilled worker, every industry is invaded. A recent report as to English nail and chain workers shows hours and general conditions to be almost intolerable, while the wage averages eightpence a day. In the mines, despite steady action concerning them, women are working by hundreds for the same rate. In short, from every quarter comes in repeated testimony that the majority of working Englishwomen are struggling for a livelihood; that a pound a week is a fortune, and that the majority live on a wage below subsistence point.

The enormous influx of foreign population is partly responsible for these conditions, but far less than is popularly supposed; since the Jews, most often accused, are in many cases juster employers than the Christians, and suffer from the same causes. For all alike, legislation is powerless to reach certain ingrained evils, and the recent sweating-commission ended its report with the words:—

> "We express the firm hope that the faithful exposure of the evils that we have been called upon to unveil, will have the effect of leading capitalists to lend greater attention to the conditions under which work is done, which furnishes the merchandise they demand. When legislation has attained the limit beyond which it can no longer be useful, the amelioration of the condition of workers can result only from the increasing moral sense of those who employ them."

This conclusion, it may be added, is in full accord with that given in the Encyclical of Pope Leo XIII., as well as with that of our most serious workers at home; our own government examination into the sweating-system, now embodied in a Congressional Report accessible to all, being simply confirmation of every point made in that for England. As a summary of many working conditions in London, I add part of a report made by an indefatigable student of social conditions, Margaret Harkness, associated now with Mr. Charles Booth, and as able an observer as her cousin and co-worker, Miss Beatrice Potter, whose report on the sweating-system makes part of Mr. Booth's first volume:[30]—

> "I have, for the last six months, been attempting to find out something about the hours and wages of girls who work at various trades in the city. Had I known how difficult the task would be, I should probably never have attempted it. Last time I heard of Mr. Besant he was sitting in his office, overwhelmed with figures and facts. He said then that he did not expect to publish anything about the work of girls and women in the United Kingdom under a year or eighteen months. I do not wonder at it. Apart from the method of his inquiry, I know how exceedingly difficult it is to arrive at the truth; the tact and patience it needs to make such investigations. Employees and employ-

ers take very different views of the same circumstances; one must listen to both, and then split the difference.

"There are at the present time absolutely no figures to go upon if one wishes to learn something about the hours and wages of girls who follow certain occupations in the city. The factory inspectors (admirable men, but very much overworked) come, with the most naive delight, to visit any person who has information to give about the people over whose interests they are supposed to watch with fatherly interest. Clergymen shake their heads, or refer one to homes and charities. One has to find out the truth for one's self. Both employers and employees must be visited. Even then one must wait days and weeks to inspire them with confidence, for thus alone can one obtain a thorough knowledge of things as they really are, and arrive at facts unbiassed by prejudice.

"So far I have found that there are, at least, two hundred trades at which girls work in the city. Some employ hundreds of hands, and some only fifty or sixty. Printers give the greatest amount of work, perhaps; but there are at least two hundred other occupations in which girls earn a living; namely, brush-makers, button-makers, cigarette-makers, electric-light fitters, fur-workers, India-rubber-stamp machinist, magic-lantern-slide makers, perfumers, portmanteau-makers, spectacle-makers, surgical-instrument makers, tie-makers, etc. These girls can be roughly divided into two classes,—those who earn from 8s. to 14s., and those who earn from 4s. to 8s. per week. Taking slack time into consideration, it is, I think, safe to say that 10s. is the average weekly wage of the first class, and 4s. 6d. that of the second class. Their weekly wage often falls below this, and sometimes rises above it. The hours are almost invariably from 8 A.M. to 7 P.M., with one hour for dinner and a half-holiday on Saturday. I know few cases in which such girls work less; a good many in which over-time reaches to ten or eleven at night; a few in which over-time means all night. There is little to choose between the two classes. The second are allowed by their employers to wear old clothes and boots; the first must make 'a genteel appearance.'

"I often hear rich women say, 'Oh, working-girls cannot be very poor; they wear such smart feathers.' If these women knew how the girls have to stint in underclothing and food in order to make what their employers call 'a genteel appearance,' I think they would pass quite another verdict. I will give two typical cases: A girl living just over Blackfriars Bridge, in one small room, for which she pays 5s., earns 10s. a week in a printer's business. She works from 8 A.M. to 6 P.M., then returns home to do all the washing, cleaning, cooking, etc., that is necessary in a one-room establishment. She has an invalid mother dependent on her efforts, and is out-patient herself at one of the London hospitals. She was sixteen last Christmas. Another girl, who lives in two cellars near Lisson Grove, with father, mother, and six brothers and sisters, earns 3s. 6d. a week in a well-known factory. She is seventeen years old, but does not look more than ten or eleven. Every morning she walks a mile to her work, arriving at eight o'clock; every evening she walks a mile back, reaching home about seven o'clock. If she arrives at the factory five minutes late, she is fined 7d. If she stays away a whole day, she is 'drilled,'—that is, kept without work a whole week. Her father has been out of employment for six months; so her weekly 3s. 6d. goes into the family purse. Her food consists of three slices of bread and butter, which she takes to the factory for dinner; one slice of bread and butter and some weak tea for supper and breakfast. These cases are not picked. They are to be found scattered all over London. Many and many a family is at the present time being kept by the labor of one or two such girls, who can at the most earn a few shillings. When one thinks what the life of a young girl is in happy families, all the joyousness of which she is capable, until sorrow sets its seal on her, one's heart aches for the sad lives of these girls in the city.

'And still her voice comes ringing

Across the soft still air,

And still I hear her singing,

"Oh, life, thou art most fair!"'

"A young girl is capable of feeling in one brief hour more intense delight than a boy of her age experiences in a fortnight. Yet all this joyousness is ruthlessly stamped upon by competition, and thousands of girls in London have no enjoyment except to gaze at monstrosities in penny gaffs, or to dance on dirty pavements; and generally these poor things are too tired even to do that. It is strange that the public take so little interest in these girls, considering they must become mothers of future citizens. 'The youth of a nation are the trustees of posterity.' What sort of daughters are these girls with their pinched faces and stunted bodies likely to give England? What will posterity say of the girl labor that now goes on in the city? I have seen strong men weeping because they have no bread to give their children; I know at the London docks chains have been replaced by wooden barriers, because starving men behind pressed so hard on starving men in front, that the latter were nearly cut in two by the iron railings; I have watched a contractor mauled when he had no work to give, and have myself been nearly killed by a brick-bat that was hurled at a contractor's head by a man whose family was starving: but I deliberately say of all the victims of our present competitive system I pity these girls the most. They are so fragile. Honest work is made for them almost impossible; and if they slip, no one gives them a second chance, they are kicked and spat upon by the public. I know that the girl-labor question is but a portion of the larger labor question, that nothing can be done for them at present; but I wish that they were not the victims of the *laissez-faire* policy in two ways instead of one; I wish that their richer sisters were not so terribly apathetic about them."

For Scotland, industries, wages, and general conditions are much the same as those of England. Factory life has been at many points improved, and the superior thrift and education of the working-class shows in the large amount of their savings. But Glasgow has faced conditions almost as terrible as those given in "The Bitter Cry of Outcast London," with a result not yet attained by the latter city, having destroyed hundreds of foul tenements to make room for improved dwellings.

For Ireland, though Irish linen, poplins, and woollens are the synonym of excellence, the proportion of women workers in these industries is comparatively small. In a few counties in the south Irish lace is made, but the women are chiefly agricultural laborers. Thanks to the efforts of Parnell, in 1885, there was formed "The Association for the Promotion of Irish Industries," then chiefly destroyed by the "Act of Union" which permitted England to levy protective tariffs on all Irish manufactures. Statistics on these points are hidden in English Blue-books, and we have no very reliable data as to the number of women and children employed. The efforts of the Countess of Aberdeen, during the term of her husband as Viceroy of Ireland, and of the Countess of Dunraven on the Dunraven estates in the county of Limerick, have done much to re-establish the lace industry,—with such success that the work compares favorably with that of some of the French convents.

In Wales, as in the North of England, women and children are employed in the mines, and there is constant evasion of the laws regulating hours, with a wage as inadequate as the work is heavy. Heavy woollens and corduroy employ a small proportion in their manufacture, wage and hours being the same as those of England.

FOOTNOTES:

[26] "The Destruction of Infants," by Mr. F.W. Lowndes, M.R.C.S., British Association for the Advancement of Science, Report for 1870, p. 586.

[27] Journal of the Statistical Society, Sept., 1870, vol. xxxiii. pp. 323-326.

[28] Parliamentary Paper, No. 372, July 20, 1871: Collected Series, vol. vii. p. 606.

[29] Sixth Report of the Medical Officer of the Privy Council, 1863, pp. 454-462. Parliamentary Paper, 1864, No. 3,416, vol. xxviii.

[30] Labor and Life of the People, vol. i.: East London. Edited by Charles Booth, p. 564.

VIII.

GENERAL CONDITIONS FOR CONTINENTAL WORKERS.

For France the census of 1847 showed a list of 959 women workers in Paris earning sixty centimes a day; 100,000 earning from sixty centimes to three francs, and 626 earning over three francs. That for 1869 showed 17,203, earning from fifty centimes to one franc twenty-five centimes daily; 11,000 of these workers being furnished lodging, food, and washing. Of the entire number 88,340 earned from one franc fifty centimes to four francs a day; 767 earned from four francs fifty centimes to ten francs daily, most of the latter class being heads of work rooms or shops. The rise in wages affected the better orders of worker, but left the sewing-woman's wage nearly unchanged. Levasseur[31] tells us that toward the end of the reign of Louis Philippe the wage of a woman varied ordinarily from twelve to twenty-five sous, exceptionally from twenty to forty; that of children being from six to fifteen sous; of men from thirty sous for ordinary laborers, to forty or forty-five for skilled work.

The census for 1851 gave for Paris 112,891 workwomen, 60,000 of whom were sewers. Convent sewing, that of the prisons and reformatories, and the competition of women who had homes and worked simply for pin-money, kept the wage at a minimum; and these conditions still operate toward that end, precisely as they do for all countries where the needle is a means of support, the evil being felt most severely in our cities. The facts in the life of a French seamstress are much the same as those of the Englishwoman. To earn two francs a day she must make eight chemises, working from fourteen to sixteen hours daily to accomplish this. The income of the average sewer does not exceed, at the best, five hundred francs, and most usually falls below. Rents are so high that a garret requires not less than one hundred francs a year. In his researches into conditions, Jules Simon[32] found that this sum compelled deprivations of every order. Expenses were as follows: Rent, 100 francs; clothing, bedding, etc., 115 francs; washing, 36 francs; heat and light, 36 francs. These sums amounted to 286.50 francs, the amount remaining for food being 215.50 or a little less than twelve sous a day,—the amount expended by two of our own seamstresses in New York in 1887, the items being given by the earner.[33]

Existence on French soil, whether in Paris, the manufacturing towns, or the provinces, has come to mean something very different from the facts of a generation ago. Then, with wages hardly above "subsistence point," the thrifty Frenchwoman not only lived, but managed to put by a trifle each month. Wages have risen, but prices have at the same time advanced. Every article of daily need is at the highest point,—sugar, which the London workwoman buys at a penny a pound, being twelve cents a pound in Paris; and flour, milk, eggs, equally high. Fuel is so dear that shivering is the law for all save the wealthy; and rents are no less dear, with no "improved dwellings" system to give the most for the scant sum at disposal. Bread and coffee, chiefly chiccory, make one meal; bread alone is the staple of the others, with a bit of meat for Sunday. Hours are frightfully long, the disabilities of the French needleworker being in many points the same as those of her English sister. In short, even skilled labor has many disabilities, the saving fact being that unskilled is in far less proportion than across the Channel, the present system of education including many forms of industrial training.

Generations of freer life than that of England, and many traditions in her favor give certain advantages to the woman born on French soil. It is taken for granted that she will after marriage share her husband's work or continue her own, and her keen intelligence is relied upon to a degree unknown to other nations. Repeated wars, and the enrolment of all her men for fixed periods of service, have developed the capacity of women in business directions, and they fill every known occupation. The light-heartedness of her nation is in her favor, and she has learned thoroughly how to extract the most from every centime. There is none of the hopeless dowdiness and dejection that characterize the lower order of Englishwoman. Trim, tidy, and thrifty, the Frenchwoman faces poverty with a smiling courage that is part of her strength, this look changing often for the older ones into a patience which still holds courage.

Thus far there is no official report of the industries in which they are engaged, and figures must be drawn from unofficial sources. M. Paul Leroy-Beaulieu, the noted political economist, in his history of "The Labor of Women in the Nineteenth Century," computes the number of women at work in the manufactories of textile fabrics, cotton, woollen, linen, and silk, as nearly one million; and outside of this is the enormous number of lace-makers and general workers in all occupations. There are over a quarter of a million of these lace-workers, whose wages run from eighty and ninety centimes to two francs a day; and the rate of payment for Swiss lace-workers is the same.

During the Congrès Féministe held in the autumn of 1892, Madame Vincent, an ardent champion of women wage-earners, presented statistics, chiefly from private sources, showing that out of 19,352,000 artisans in France, there are 4,415,000 women who receive in wages or dividends nearly $500,000,000 a year. Their wage is much less in proportion to the work they do than that of men, yet they draw thirty-five per cent of the entire sum spent in wages. In Paris alone, over 8,000 women are doing business on an independent footing; and of 3,858 suits judged in 1892 by the Workingman's Council, 1,674 concerned women. In spite of these numbers and the abuses known to exist, the Chamber of Deputies has refused practically to extend to women workers the law for the regulation of the conditions of work in workshops. The refusal is disguised under the form of adjournment of the matter, the reason assigned being that the grievances of women are by no means ripe enough for discussion. Women themselves are not at all of the same mind; and the result has already been a move toward definite organization of trades, and united action for all women engaged in them,—a step hitherto regarded as impossible. The first effect of this has been a protest from Paris shopgirls against the action of the Chamber of Deputies, and the formation of committees whose business will be to enlist the interest and co-operation of women throughout the entire country,—a slow process, but one that will mean both education and final release from some at least of the worst disabilities now weighting all women workers.

"La femme devenue ouvrière, n'est plus une femme," wrote Jules Simon in a burst of despair at the conditions of the Paris workwoman; and he repeated the word as his investigations extended to manufacturing France, and he found everywhere the home in many cases abolished, the *crèche* taking its place till the child, vitally dependent upon a care that included love, gave up the struggle for existence, rendering its tiny quota to the long list of infant mortality. M. Leroy-Beaulieu had described years before the practical extinction of the family and the government interference[34] brought about by the discoveries made by the government inspecting committee, upon whom consternation seized as they found decadence of morals, enfeebled physique, and that the ordinary girl-worker at sixteen or seventeen could not sew a seam, or make a broth, or care for a child's needs or the simplest demands of a home. Appalled at these conditions, France set about the organization of industrial schools, and these have altered the whole face of affairs.

Generations of abuses had made, up to the time of the investigation, the history of the working-class in France. One of their best-known scientific observers, the statistician Villermé, examined in person, and as one of the government inspecting committee reported on the condition of dwellings in Lille, Amiens, and other manufacturing towns of France. The weavers and spinners of Lille lived in caves, of which thirty-six hundred were found occupied by families,—father, mother, and children as soon as old enough, employed in the mills, and returning at night to these dens, where filth and darkness periodically did their work of decimation, and where infant mortality had reached the maximum. Horrified at the discoveries made, three thousand of these dwellings were at once destroyed. But for unknown and quite inscrutable reasons six hundred were allowed to remain and receive double the original number of tenants.[35] Years passed before the last cave was filled up, the children born in them providing an enormous percentage for prison and galleys. At Douai, Rouen, Roubaix, and many other points, such hideous filth marked the homes of the working-class that Villermé reported: "The walls are covered with a thousand layers of ordure." The women, exhausted and depleted by a day's labor of from twelve to fourteen hours, had no time to think of cleanliness. In fact, its meaning had never been taught; and though industrial schools increase, hours are now shortened, and inspection is active, it remains true that almost the same conditions perpetuate themselves at many points,—the descriptions given by the great realist, Zola, of women and children in the mines, and the hideousness of their home life, being very literal and unexaggerated fact.

As to conditions of the work itself, many trades and occupations require for their proper carrying on methods and surroundings absolutely destructive to health. In all preparation of hemp and oakum dust is excessive; far beyond that of the cotton-mill, which itself breeds consumption. In the spinning of flax great heat and water are both necessities. "Nothing is more wretched," writes Jules Simon, "than a linen-spinner's surroundings. Water covers the brick floor. The odor of the linen and a temperature often exceeding twenty-five Reaumur fill the workroom with an intolerable stench. The majority of the workwomen, obliged to put off most of their garments, are huddled together in this pestilential atmosphere, imprisoned in the machines, pressed one against the other, their bodies streaming with sweat, their feet bare to the ankle; and when a day, nominally of twelve hours but really of thirteen and a half, is over, they quit the workroom for home, the rags they wear barely protecting them from cold and damp."

Details of the same order abound in the work of the political economist M. Leroy-Beaulieu,[36] who seeks at all points to give the most favorable impression possible. In each and every case the great authorities appear to be of one mind as to the disastrous effects upon the children born to these mothers. That the *crèche* is now practically a part of every factory makes little or no difference.

"The *crèche*," writes Jules Simon, "abolishes maternity in all save its pains. The working mother is defrauded of her own means of growth, bound up in the training of the child; and the child loses its right to be loved and guarded by love." In short, for all continental countries, as well as for England and our women, the question of child labor and the destiny of the child are inextricably bound up in that of the working mother, and are vital factors in working out the problem of woman as a wage-earner. What proportion of wage-earning women recruit the ranks of prostitution, is a question often asked. In Paris, which is in one sense the focus of French labor, its many opportunities drawing to it a large contingent from the provinces, it is popularly supposed that the ranks of the sewing-women give large proportion to houses of prostitution. This opinion is the prevailing one for all large cities, whether in Europe or America, yet is disproved on all sides. For Paris Parent-Duchalet states that in the statistics given by the prefecture of police, in a table including forty-one categories, women with no occupation had first rank as prostitutes, domestic service giving the second, and sewing-women the smallest proportion. This is the more surprising when one considers that their wage is often below the point of subsistence, and that temptation of every order waits upon them. At the best the wage falls far below that of men, even when both engage in the same work. The present movement toward organization is the first step toward a general bettering of all trades and their wage; and for fullest details of this, and work in connection with the admirable Bourse du Travail, one of its most important features of working life to-day in Paris, the reader must turn to the reports themselves, beginning with the first one, issued in 1887-88.[37] The same facts may be said to form the story of labor in Belgium, in Switzerland, in Italy, and at all points where women or children are at work, whether in factory or mine or workshop. For Belgium the situation is summed up in a very important and minute report of the government inquiry commission into the labor of women and children,—the first made in 1867 and followed by one in 1874, the latest having been made in 1891.[38]

A comprehensive law, promulgated Nov. 2, 1892, and regulating the labor of women and children in factories and mines, was amended in May, 1893, by the addition of very specific regulations as to all employments affecting health and morals. The Presidential decree consists of two parts, — the first dealing with the employment of women and children in connection with machinery when in motion, or in which the dangerous parts are not fully protected, in glass-blowing and in carrying weights. The second part of the decree consists of three tables, of which A enumerates certain industries, chiefly the manufacture of acids, dyes, chemicals, etc., also manures and glass, crystal, and metal polishing, in which female and child labor are prohibited; B those in which children under eighteen must not work, chiefly the manufacture of explosives; and C, a large variety of other industries in which female and child labor is only allowed conditionally. The great majority of these are industries involving special risk through the disengagement of dust-particles or vapors; while a few are ranked as dangerous, owing to risk of fire and the contraction of special diseases, etc.

Belgium, French in feeling and in methods, has known some of the worst abuses discoverable on continental soil, thousands of women and children in her mines having toiled from twelve to sixteen hours a day, with often no Sunday rest, for a wage at bare subsistence point. In "Germinal," Zola, who spent months observing every phase of their life, has given a picture, unsurpassed in any literature, of the misery and degradation of the worker. An investigation in 1874, and indignation at some of the conditions then discovered, brought about modifications of the law. That of the general congress of 1891 accomplished much more; but work must still be done before any very marked advance becomes discernible.

Passing to Germany, a good two-thirds of the women are at work in field or shop or home, the proportion of women in agriculture being larger than in any other country of Europe. Her schools furnish better training than those of any other nation. In all these points Prussia leads, though till recently legislation has been in behalf of child-workers, and women have been practically ignored. But factory regulations are minute and extended; and the questions involved in the labor of women, and its bearing on health, longevity, etc., are now coming under consideration. In Silesia, as early as

1868, women were excluded from the salt-mines; and the Labor Congress of 1889 brought about many changes of the laws on this point for Belgium and Germany. In Italy, in which country industrial education is now receiving much attention, the labor of women, continuous, severe, and underpaid, as it is known to be, finds small mention, save among special students of social questions. Russia has practically no data from which judgment can be formed. In short, it is only in English-speaking countries that really efficient action as to the labor of women has taken place; while even for them the work has but begun, and new and more radical forms will be necessary for any real progress toward final betterment. Toward such end the labor bureaus of our own country are working diligently; and it is with them that we have next to do, the investigations already made and incorporated in their reports being full of suggestion for future workers.

The census of 1882 gave for Germany, in a population of 45,222,113 persons, 23,071,364 women, of whom 1,109,530 were widows, and 5,467,730 unmarried, a large proportion of both these classes being self-supporting. An immense number of these were agricultural laborers. In Prussia in 1867 the census gave the number of women agricultural laborers as 1,054,213. Woman's wage for a day's labor, always twelve and often fourteen hours, is from twenty to twenty-five cents, about a third of that received by men doing the same work. Brassey, the great railroad contractor, found throughout Germany that her wage was always a third and often a quarter less than that of men.

For united Germany the description given by Villermé in 1836 is still true for many points. "The misery in which the cotton spinners and weavers of the upper Rhine live," he writes, "is so profound that it produces the saddest results. In the families of manufacturers, drapers, merchants, etc., half the children born attain their nineteenth year, this same half ceasing to exist before the age of two years in the families of weavers and workers at cotton-spinning."

As to numbers employed in trades and industries, it is difficult to secure them with exactness. The census of 1871 reported three tenths of the population as agricultural, the males employed in agriculture being 2,338,174, and the females 4,426,573. Household service had 840,000 women on its rolls. In 1875 the cotton-mills employed in weaving and spinning 95,934 women; the woollen manufacture, nearly 193,000; linen, hemp, and jute, 190,000. The labor of women and children was hardly recognized, and statistics had to be disentangled as best they might be from general tables of occupations. Through the persistent efforts of the Centre in the German Reichstag, a gradual betterment of the working-classes has been brought about, and thus indirectly that of women and children,— the first combined and determined effort being made in 1889, when three bills were brought up for discussion. The first made the working-day not to exceed eleven hours; the second demanded the suspension of industrial labor on Sunday, save in exceptional cases, when five hours' labor was to be allowed; the third concerned the labor of women and children, and with some modifications is practically the law to-day. Night and Sunday labor in mines, smelting-works, rolling-mills, and dockyards is entirely forbidden, nor can married women work more than ten hours a day. The Federal Council has the right also to forbid the employment of women and children in all factories and establishments where health and morals are exposed to exceptional dangers.

At the period at which the investigations which brought about the agitation of the question were made, the number of child laborers had increased in two years from 155,000 to 192,000, children hardly more than babies being in the factories. At present the law forbids the employment of any child under twelve, and not less than three hours' schooling daily is compulsory. Abuses exist at all points, women workers in mines faring, even with shortened day, in very evil case,—the wage at or below subsistence point and the general conditions of the most hopeless order. Constant agitation goes on in the Reichstag, and organization among the women themselves will in time bring about needed reforms; but as a whole the German woman is in many points less considered than the women of any other civilized nation.

Though Italy is pre-eminently an agricultural country, and men, women, and children are alike employed in agricultural pursuits, there has been no trustworthy record of numbers engaged. In manufacturing there are more statistics, but interest in the woman's share in labor is of recent date. In the silk manufacture, in which

Italy ranks second only to China, and far beyond all other competitors, 81,165 women and 25,373 children were employed in 1877, chiefly in unwinding cocoons, the number at present having increased nearly ten per cent. In the cotton industry there were employed, at the time of the same census, 2,696 women and 2,520 children; and a proportionate increase in numbers has taken place. In the flax and hemp industries nearly seventy thousand workers used hand-looms at home, the larger proportion of these being women. In the factories it was found that 2,565 women and 1,227 children were at work as spinners, and 3,394 women and 1,020 children as weavers. Women are steadily employed in the manufacture of straw hats and bonnets, in jute in many forms, in cigar and cigarette making, and in many other industries, cheap clothing leading. Of the thirty millions and more of population, not quite half are women; and of these nearly half are wage-earners, the majority in unrecorded forms of labor,—chiefly household service or the care of their own homes, with some petty industry adding its mite to the yearly income. But industrial training has but begun for Italy. The wage is pitiably low, the conditions of living hard and full of privation; nor can these facts alter till better education and organization have been brought about. The latest Italian census is not yet published; but proofs of tables of the comparative wage for twenty years in some of the principal industries have been sent me through the courtesy of Signor Luigi Bodio, the minister of agriculture, commerce, and general statistics. From these tables it is found that the daily wage of women cotton-spinners has risen from sixty centimes, in 1871, to one franc twenty-six centimes in 1891, this being the equivalent of one lire twenty-six centissimi. The wage for weaving has risen from eighty centimes, in 1871, to one franc twenty-six centimes in 1891. Spoolers in 1871 received eighty-eight centimes as against one franc thirty centimes in 1891. In hemp-spinning the wage has fallen from ninety to eighty centimes, but has risen from ninety-eight centimes to one franc thirty centimes for twisting; the wage in the cases cited being a little more than a third that of men. In paper-making experienced workers now receive one franc fifty-two centimes as against sixty-six centimes in 1871; and in making of stearine candles one franc as against seventy-eight centimes in 1871. Running through the tables of every industry, the average is about the same,—the wage for women, even when doing the same work, hardly more than a third that for men, and the amount for either at bare subsistence point.

In Russia the woman's wage is but a fifth that of men, with working conditions, save at a few points where the work of Professor Janzhul and his confrères has told, at the very worst, — the day being from twelve to sixteen hours long even in the best-managed factories, while in the village industries, which, owing to the peculiar conditions of Russian life, make up the larger proportion of her industries, it is for many workers almost unending, the merest respite being given for sleep. As yet but few authentic figures as to the numbers employed are given, though on the first investigation into domestic industries made a few years since it was found that over 890,000 were engaged in them, and also at the same time in agriculture. Manufacturing in Russia concentrates about Moscow and St. Petersburg, which represent more than two fifths of the whole production of the empire. The requirements of nine tenths of the Russian people are met by domestic manufacture in the villages, and home-weaving for the market employs over two hundred thousand workers, other textiles, leather, etc., being dealt with in the same way.

In the other northern countries of Europe, — Norway, Sweden, and Denmark, — manufactures are at a minimum, fisheries and agriculture being the chief industries. Women are employed in both; and in the few factories there is a small proportion of women and children, working at a wage much less than that given to men. Sweden has a most admirable system of industrial education; and Norway and Denmark, though far less in population, have adopted the same methods. But the limitations of all wage-earning women are felt here in the same manner as elsewhere, the summary for all countries being much the same. The Northern workwoman has the advantage of training and of as keen a sense of economy as the Frenchwoman; but her wage is most usually at or below subsistence point, and her difficulties are those of the worker in general, — long hours, insufficient pay, and fierce competition.

As to the present laws concerning the length of the working-day, a general abstract is found in a return issued in reply to an address from the House of Commons, an abstract of which was given in "St. James' Gazette": —

"In France the hours of adult labor are regulated by a series of decrees, of which the earliest, promulgated September, 1848, enacts that the working-man's day in manufactories and mills shall not exceed twelve hours of 'effective' or actual labor. A decree issued in May, 1851, made exceptions, so that more hours might be worked in certain trades. In 1885 a circular was issued stating that the limit of twelve hours *per diem* was not to be imposed where hand-power was employed, but was to be confined to manufactories and mills in which the motive power was machinery. No workshops were to come under the clauses of the act that did not employ more than twenty hands in any one shed. The report says: 'It is likewise to be borne in mind that there is in France no compulsory observance of Sunday, and no day of habitual rest.'

"The reports of the French inspectors of labor appear to show that the Act of 1848 is very loosely interpreted. It is even doubtful whether the section limiting the actual working-day to twelve hours was intended to include or exclude hours of rest. Practically the legal time is made to exclude rest. This makes the working-day so much the longer. Thus one of the French inspectors states that the hours of attendance in factories under the Act of 1848 are from five in the morning until seven in the evening, or a total of fourteen hours, out of which there are twelve hours of 'effective labor.' But the same authority also states that 'effective' time often extends to thirteen and fourteen hours in many weaving-establishments. Finally, we are told that, as a rule, it may be taken that Frenchmen employed in factories are present in the shops at least fourteen hours out of every twenty four.

"Among the countries having no laws affecting the hours of adult labor, Germany is conspicuous. Employers, however, cannot force their servants to work on Sundays and feast-days. Employment of youthful or female labor in certain kinds of factories, which is attended with special danger to health or morals, is forbidden, or made conditional on certain regulations, by which night labor for female work-people is especially forbidden. In Germany, as in other countries also, women may not be employed in factories for a certain time after childbirth. In Hesse-Darmstadt the medium duration of labor is from ten to twelve hours,—the cases in which the latter time is exceeded being, however, more frequent than those in which the former is not exceeded. The normal work-day throughout Saxony in all the principal branches of industry is from 6 A.M. to 7 P.M., with half an hour for breakfast, an hour for dinner, and half an hour for supper. In the manufacturing industry there are departures from these hours, the period of work in spinning and weaving mills not infrequently being twelve hours.

"In Austria the law provides that the duration of work for factory hands shall not exceed eleven hours out of the twenty-four, 'exclusive' of the periods of rest. These are not to be less in the aggregate than an hour and a half. The rule can be modified by the minister of commerce, in conjunction with the minister of the interior, allowing longer hours. The hours have been so extended to twelve hours in certain industries, such as spinning-mills, and even to thirteen in silk manufactories. Sunday rest is enforced. In Hungary there is no limit laid down by law, but the hours are not generally longer than in Austria.

"Concerning the actual hours of adult labor in Belgium, some difficulty is said to be experienced in getting at the facts. The evidence given before a Belgian royal commission showed that railway guards are sometimes on duty for fifteen and even nineteen and a half hours at a stretch; and the Brussels tram-way-drivers are at work from fifteen to seventeen hours daily, with a rest of only an hour and a half at noon. Brick-makers work during the summer months sixteen hours a day. In the sugar refineries the average hours are from twelve to thirteen for men and from nine to ten for women. The cabinetmakers, both at Ghent and Brussels, assert that they have often to work seventeen hours a day.

"In Switzerland the law provides that a normal working-day shall not exceed eleven hours, reduced on Saturdays and public holidays to ten. Power is reserved for prolonging the working-day in certain circumstances. Except in cases of absolute necessity Sunday labor is prohibited, and in establishments where uninterrupted labor is required, each working hand must have one free Sunday out of two. Women cannot under any circumstances be employed in night or Sunday labor. Italy has not legislated for adults, but has made regulations for child labor. Sweden is in the same position. Spain and Portugal have done nothing. The general rule in the latter country, applying to old and young, is to work from sunrise to sunset, an hour and a half being allowed for meals. In the Netherlands a law was recently promulgated to prevent excessive and dangerous work by grown-up women and young persons. In Turkey the working-day lasts from sunrise to sunset, with certain intervals for repose and refreshment. In Russia, where there are no laws affecting the hours of adult labor, the normal working-day in industrial establishments averages twelve hours, though it is often extended to fourteen and even sixteen."

FOOTNOTES:

[31] Histoire des Classes Ouvriers en France depuis 1789 jusqu'à nos Jours, par E. Levasseur.

[32] L'Ouvrière, par Jules Simon.

[33] Prisoners of Poverty, p. 118.

[34] Le Travail des Femmes au XIX. Siècle, par Paul Leroy-Beaulieu.

[35] L'Ouvrière, p. 158.

[36] Le Travail des Femmes aux XIX. Siècle.

[37] Annuaire de la Bourse du Travail. Volumes from 1887 to 1892 inclusive.

[38] Rapport sur l'Enquête faite au nom de l'Académie Royale de Médecine de Belgique, par la commission chargée d'étudier la question de l'emploi des femmes dans les travaux souterrain des mines, Bruxelles, 1868.

Documents nouveaux relatifs au travail des femmes et des enfants, dans les manufactures, les mines, etc, etc. Bruxelles, 1874.

CHAPTER IX.

GENERAL CONDITIONS AMONG WAGE-EARNING WOMEN IN THE UNITED STATES.

The summary already made of the work of bureaus of labor and their bearing upon women wage-earners includes some points belonging under this head which it still seemed advisable to leave where they stand. The work of the Massachusetts Bureau gave the keynote, followed by all successors, and thus required full outlining; and it is from that, as well as successors, that general conditions are to be determined. A brief summary of such facts as each State has investigated and reported upon will be given, with the final showing of the latest and most general report, — that from the United States Bureau of Labor for 1889.

Beginning with New England and taking State by State in the usual geographical order, that of Maine for 1888 leads. Work here was done by a special commissioner appointed for the purpose, and the chief towns and cities in the State were visited. No occupation was excluded. The foreign element of the State is comparatively small. There is no city in which overcrowding and its results in the tenement-house system are to be found. Factories are numerous, and the bulk of Maine working-women are found in them; the canning industry employs hundreds, and all trades have their proportion of workers. For all of them conditions are better in many ways than at almost any other point in New England, many of them living at home and paying but a small proportion of their wages toward the family support.

A large proportion of the factories have boarding-houses attached, which are run by a contractor. A full inspection of these was made, and the report pronounces them to be better kept than the ordinary boarding-house, with liberal dietary and comfortable rooms. Many of the women owned their furniture, and had made "homes" out of the narrow quarters. These were the better-paid class of workers. Several of the factories have "Relief Associations," in which the employees pay a small sum weekly, which secures them a fixed sum during illness or disability. The conditions, as a whole, in factory are more nearly those of Massachusetts during the early days of the Lowell mills than can be found elsewhere.

Taking the State as a whole, though the average wage is nearly a dollar less a week than that of Massachusetts, its buying power is somewhat more, from the fact that rents are lower and the conditions of living simpler, though this is true only of remote towns.

Massachusetts follows; and here, as in Maine, there is general complaint that many of the girls live at home, pay little or no board, and thus can take a lower wage than the self-supporting worker. In the large stores employees are hired at the lowest possible figure; and many girls who are working for from four to five dollars per week state that it is impossible to pay for room and board with even tolerably decent clothing. Hundreds who want pin-money do work at a price impossible to the self-supporting worker, many married women coming under this head; and bitter complaint is made on this point. At the best the wage is at a minimum, and only the most rigid economy renders it possible for the earner to live on it. That there is not greater suffering reflects all honor on the army of hardworking women, pronounced by the commissioner to be as industrious, moral, and virtuous a class as the community owns.

"Homes" of every order have been established in Boston and in other large towns in the State; and as they give board at the lowest rate, they are filled with girls. They are rigid as to rules and regulations, and not in favor, as a rule, with the majority. A very slight relaxing of lines and more effort to make them cheerful would result in bringing many who now remain outside; but in any case they can reach but a small proportion.

In unskilled labor there is little difference among the workers. All alike are half starved, half clothed, overworked to a frightful degree; the report specifying numbers whose day's work runs from fourteen to sixteen hours, and with neither time to learn some better method of earning a living, nor hope enough to spur them on in any new path. This class is found chiefly among sewing-women on cheap clothing, bags, etc.; and there is no present means of reaching them or altering the conditions which surround them.

Connecticut factories are subject to the same general laws as those governing like work in Maine and Massachusetts. Over thirty thousand women and girls are engaged in factory work, and ten thousand children,—chiefly girls, women being twenty-five per cent of all employed in factories. Legislation has lessened or abolished altogether some of the worst features of this life, and there are special mills which have won the highest reputation for just dealing and care of every interest of their employees. But the same reasons that affect general conditions for all workers exist here also, and produce the same results, not only in factory labor, but in all other industries open to women. The fact that there are no large cities, and thus little overcrowding in tenements, and that there is home life for a large proportion of the workers, tells in their favor. Factory boardinghouses fairly well kept abound; but the average wage, $6.50, is a trifle lower than that of Massachusetts, and implies more difficulty in making ends meet. Many of the worst abuses in child labor arose in Connecticut, and the reports for both 1885 and 1886 state that for both women and children much remains to be done. Clothing here, as elsewhere, is synonymous with overwork and underpay, the wage being below subsistence point; and want of training is often found to be a portion of the reason for these conditions.

In Rhode Island, as in all the New England States, the majority of the factories are in excellent condition, the older ones alone being open to the objections justly made both by employees and the reports of the Labor Bureau. The wage falls below that of Connecticut, while the general conditions of living are practically the same, the statements made as to the first applying with equal force to the last. Manufactures are the chief employment, the largest number of women workers being found in these. Of all of them the commissioner reports: "They work harder and more hours than men, and receive much less pay."[39] The fact of no large cities, and thus no slums, is in the worker's favor; but limitations are in all other points sharp and continuous.

New York follows, and for the State at large the same remarks apply at every point. It is New York City in which focuses every evil that hedges about women workers, and in a degree not to be found at any other portion of the country. These will be dealt with in the proper place. The average wage, so far as the State is concerned, gives the same result as those already mentioned. Manufacturing gives large employment; and this is under as favorable conditions as in New England, though the average wage is nearly a dollar less than that of Massachusetts, while expenses are in some ways higher. The incessant tide of foreign labor tends steadily to lower the wage-rate, and the struggle for mere subsistence is the fact for most.

In New York City, while there is a large proportion of successful workers, there is an enormous mass of the lowest order. No other city offers so varied a range of employment, and there is none where so large a number are found earning a wage far below the "life limit."

The better-paying trades are filled with women who have had some form of training in school or home, or have passed from one occupation to another, till that for which they had most aptitude has been determined. That, however, to which all the more helpless turn at once, as the one thing about the doing of which there can be no doubt or difficulty, is the one most over-crowded, most underpaid, and with its scale of payments lessening year by year. The girl too ignorant to reckon figures, too dull-witted to learn by observation, takes refuge in sewing in one of its many forms as the one thing possible to all grades of intelligence; often the need of work for older women arises from the death or evil habits of the natural head of the family, and fortunes have sunk to so low an ebb that at times the only clothing left is on the back of the worker in the last stages of demoralization. Employment in a respectable place thus becomes impossible, and the sole method of securing work is through the middlemen or sweaters, who ask no questions and require no reference, but make as large a profit as can be wrung from the helplessness and bitter need of those with whom they reckon.

The difficulties to be faced by the woman whose only way of self-support is limited to the needle, whether in machine or handwork, are fourfold: first, her own incompetency must very often head the list, and prevent her from securing first-class work; second, middlemen or sweaters lower the price to starvation point; third, contract work done in prisons or reformatories brings about the same result; and fourth, she is underbid from still another quarter,—that of the countrywoman living at home, who takes the work at any price offered.

The Report of the New York Bureau of Labor for 1885 contains a mass of evidence so fearful in its character, and demonstrating conditions of life so tragic for the worker, and so shameful on the part of the employer, that general attention was for the time aroused. It is impossible here to make more than this general statement referring all readers to the report itself for full detail. Thousands herded together in tenement houses and received a daily wage of from twenty-five to sixty cents, the day's labor being often sixteen hours long. "The Bitter Cry of Outcast London" found its parallel here, nor has there been any diminution of the numbers involved, though at some points conditions have been improved. But the facts recorded in the report are practically the same to-day; and the income of many workers falls below two dollars a week, from which sum food, clothing, light, fuel, and rent are to be provided for. The sum and essence of every wrong and injustice that can hedge about the worker is found at this point, and remains a problem to every worker among the poor, the solving of which will mean the solution of the whole labor question.

New Jersey reports have from the beginning followed the phases of the labor movement with a keen intelligence and interest. They give general conditions as much the same as those of New York State. The wage-rate is but $5; and Newark especially, a city which is filled with manufacturing establishments of every order, reproduces some of the evil conditions of New York City, though in far less degree. Taking the State as a whole, legislation has done much to protect the worker, and other reforms are persistently urged by the bureau. They are needed. In the official report of conditions among the linen-thread spinners of Paterson we find: "In one branch of this industry women are compelled to stand on a stone floor in water the year round, most of the time barefoot, with a spray of water from a revolving cylinder flying constantly against the breast; and the coldest night in winter, as well as the warmest in summer, these poor creatures must go to their homes with water dripping from their underclothing along their path, because there could not be space or a few moments allowed them wherein to change their clothing."[40]

Thus much for the East; and we turn to the West, where some of the most practical and suggestive forms of investigation are now in full operation.

FOOTNOTES:

[39] Third Annual Report of the Commissioner of Industrial Statistics of Rhode Island, 1889, p. 22.

[40] Report of the Bureau of Labor for the State of New Jersey, 1888.

X.

GENERAL CONDITIONS IN THE WESTERN STATES.

The reports from Kansas and Wisconsin give a wage but slightly above that of New Jersey, the weekly average being $5.27. Of the 50,000 women at work in 1889,—the number having now nearly doubled,—but 6,000 were engaged in manufacturing, the larger portion being in domestic service. Save in one or two of the larger towns and cities, there is no overcrowding, and few of the conditions that go with a denser population and sharper competition. Kansas gives large space to general conditions, and, while urging better pay, finds that her working-women are, as a whole, honest, self-respecting, moral members of the community. Factory workers are few in proportion to those in other occupations; and this is true of most of the Western States, where general industries are found rather than manufactures.

The report from Colorado for 1889 includes in its own returns certain facts discovered on investigation in Ohio and Indiana, and matched by some of the same nature in Colorado. The methods of Eastern competition had been adopted, and Commissioner Rice reports: —

> "In one of the large cities of Ohio the labor commissioners of that State discovered that shirts were being made for 36 cents a dozen; and that the rules of one establishment paying such wages employing a large number of females, required that the

day's labor should commence and terminate with
prayer and thanksgiving."

In Indiana matters appear even worse. By personal investigation, it was found that the following rates of wages were being paid in manufacturing establishments in Indianapolis: For making shirts, 30 to 60 cents a dozen; overalls, 40 to 60 cents a dozen pairs; pants, 50 cents to $1.25 per dozen pairs. "In our own State," writes the commissioner, "owing to Eastern competition on the starvation wage plan, are found women and girls working for mere subsistence, though the prices paid here are a shade higher. It is found that shirts are made at 80 cents a dozen, and summer dresses from 25 cents upward."

Prices are higher here than at almost any other portion of the United States, and thus the wage gives less return. In spite of the general impression that women fare well at this point, the report gives various details which seem to prove abuses of many orders. It made special investigation into the conditions of domestic service, that in hotels and large boarding-houses being found to be full of abuses, though conditions as a whole were favorable. In so new a State there are few manufacturing interests; and the factories investigated are many of them reported as showing an almost criminal disregard of the comfort and interests of the employees. Aside from this, the report indicates much the same general conditions as prevail in other States.

In Minnesota, with its average wage of $6 per week, there are few factories,—manufacturing being confined to clothing, boots and shoes, and a few other forms. Domestic service has the largest number of women employed, and stores and trades absorb the remainder. There is no overcrowding save here and there in the cities, as in St. Paul or Minneapolis, where girls often club together in rooming. While many of the workers are Scandinavian, many are native born; and for the latter there is often much thrift and a comfortable standard of living. The same complaints as to lowness of wage, resulting from much the same causes as those specified elsewhere, are heard; and in the clothing manufacture wages are kept at the lowest possible point As a whole, the returns indicate more comfort than in Colorado, but leave full room for betterment. The chapter on "Domestic Service" shows many strong reasons why girls prefer factory or general work to this; and as the views of heads of employment agencies are also given, unusual opportunity is afforded for forming just judgment in the matter.

Next on the list comes the report from California for 1887 and 1888. The resources of the bureau were so limited that it was impossible to obtain returns for the whole State, and the commissioner therefore limited his inquiry to a thorough investigation of the working-women of San Francisco, in number about twenty thousand. The State has but one cotton-mill, but there are silk, jute, woollen, corset, and shirt factories, with many minor industries. Home and general sanitary conditions were all investigated, the bureau following the general lines pursued by all.

Wages are considered at length; and Commissioner Tobin states that the rate paid to women in California "does not compare favorably with the rates paid to women in the Eastern States, as do the wages of men, for the reason that Chinese come more into competition with women than with men. This is especially the case among seamstresses, and in nearly all our factories ... in other lines of labor the wages paid to females in this State are generally higher than elsewhere."

Rent, food, and clothing cost more in California than in the Eastern States. The wage-tables show that the tendency is to limit a woman's wage to a dollar a day, even in the best paid trades, and as much below this as labor can be obtained.

In shirt-making, Commissioner Tobin states that she is worse off than in any of the Eastern States. Clothing of all orders pays as little as possible, the best workwomen often making not over $2.87 per week. Even at these starvation rates, girls prefer factory work to domestic service; and as this phase was also investigated, we have another chapter of most valuable and suggestive information. In spite of low wages and all the hardship resulting, working women and girls as a whole are found to be precisely what the reports state them to be,—hard-working, honest, and moral members of the community. General conditions are much the same as those of Colorado, the summary for all the States from which reports have come being that the average wage is insufficient to allow of much more than mere subsistence.

The labor reports for the State of Missouri for 1889 and 1890 do not deal directly with the question of women wage-earners; but indirectly much light is thrown by the investigation, in that for 1889, into the cost of living and the home conditions of many miners and workers in general trades; while that for 1890 covers a wider field, and gives, with general conditions for all workers, detailed information as to many frauds practised upon them. The commissioner, Lee Merriweather, is so identified with the interests of the worker, whether man or woman, that a formal report from him on women wage-earners would have had especial value.

Last on the list of State reports comes an admirable one from Michigan, prepared by Labor Commissioner Henry A. Robinson, issued in February, 1892, which devotes nearly two hundred pages to women wage-earners, and gives careful statistics of 137 different trades and 378 occupations. Personal visits were made to 13,436 women and girls living in the most important manufacturing towns and cities of the State; and the blanks, which were prepared in the light of the experience gained by the work of other bureaus, contained 129 questions, classified as follows: social, 28; industrial, 12; hours of labor, 14; economic, 54; sanitary, 21; and seven other questions as to dress, societies, church attendance, with remarks and suggestions by the women workers. The result is a very minute knowledge of general conditions, the series of tables given being admirably prepared. In those on the hours of labor it is found that domestic service exacts the greatest number of hours; one class returning fourteen hours as the rule. In this lies a hint of the increasing objection to domestic service,—longer hours and less freedom being the chief counts against it. The final summary gives the average wage for the State as $4.86; the highest weekly average for women workers employed as teachers or in public positions being $10.78.

The remarks and suggestions of the women themselves are extraordinarily helpful. Outside the cities organization among them is unknown; but it is found that those trades which are organized furnish the best paid and most intelligent class of girls, who con-

ceived at once the benefits of a labor bureau, and answered fully
and promptly. The hours of work in all industries ranged from nine
to ten, and the wage paid was found to be a little more than fifty per
cent less than that of men engaged in the same work. A large proportion supported relatives, and general conditions as to living
were of much the same order of comfort and discomfort as those
given in other reports. The fact that this report is the latest on this
subject, and more minute in detail than has before been possible,
makes it invaluable to the student of social conditions; and it is en-
tertaining reading, even for the average reader.

We come now to the final report, in some ways a summary of
all,—that of the United States Labor Department at Washington,
and the work for 1889.

In the twenty-two cities investigated by the agents of this bureau,
the average age at which girls began work was found to be 15 years
and 4 months. Charleston, S.C., gives the highest average, it being
there 18 years and 7 months, and Newark, N.J., the lowest,—14
years and 7 months. The average period in which all had been engaged in their present occupations is shown to be 4 years and 9
months; while of the total number interviewed, 9,540 were engaged
in their first attempt to earn a living.

As against the opinion often expressed that foreign workers are in
the majority, we find that of the whole number given, 14,120 were
native born. Of the foreign born, Ireland is most largely represented,
having 936; and Germany comes next, with 775. In the matter of
parentage, 12,907 had foreign-born mothers. The number of single
women included in the report is 15,387; 745 were married, and 2,038
widowed, from which it is evident that, as a rule, it is single women
who are fighting the industrial fight alone. They are not only sup-
porting themselves, but are giving their earnings largely to the support of others at home. More than half—8,754—do this; and 9,813,
besides their occupation, help in the home housekeeping. Of the
total number, 4,928 live at home, but only 701 of them receive aid or
board from their families. The average number in these families is
5.25, and each contains 2.48 workers.

Concerning education, church attendance, home and shop conditions, 15,831 reported. Of these, 10,458 were educated in American

public schools, and 5,375 in other schools; 5,854 attend Protestant churches; 7,769 the Catholic, and 367 the Hebrew. A very large percentage, comprehending 3,209, do not attend church at all.

In home conditions 12,120 report themselves as "comfortable," while 4,692 give home conditions as "poor." "Poor," to the ordinary observer, is to be interpreted as wretched, including overcrowding, and all the numberless evils of tenement-house life, which is the portion of many. A side light is thrown on personal characteristics of the workers, in the tables of earnings and lost time. Out of 12,822 who reported, 373 earn less than $100 a year, and this class has an average of 86.5 lost days for the year covered by the investigation. With the increase of earnings, the lost time decreases, the 2,147 who earn from $200 to $450 losing but 37.8; while 398, earning from $350 to $500 a year, lost but 18.3 days.

Deliberate cruelty and injustice on the part of the employer are encountered only now and then; but competition forces the working in as inexpensive a manner as possible, and thus often makes what must sum up as cruelty and injustice necessary to the continued existence of the employer as an industrial factor. Home conditions are seldom beyond tolerable, and very often intolerable. Inspection,—the efficiency of which has greatly increased,—the demand by the organized charities at all points for women inspectors, and the gradual growth of popular interest are bringing about a few improvements, and will bring more; but the mass everywhere are as stated. Ignorance and the vices that accompany ignorance—want of thoroughness, unpunctuality, thriftlessness, and improvidence—are all in the count against the lowest order of worker; but the better class, and indeed the large proportion of the lower, are living honest, self-respecting, infinitely dreary lives.

It is a popular belief, already referred to elsewhere, that the working-women form a large proportion of the numbers who fill houses of prostitution; and that "night-walkers" are made up chiefly from the same class. Nothing could be further from the truth,—the testimony of the fifteenth annual report of the Massachusetts Bureau of Labor being in the same line as that of all in which investigation of the subject has been made, and all confirming the opinion given. The investigation of the Massachusetts Bureau in fourteen cities showed clearly that a very small proportion among working-women entered this life. The largest number, classed by occupations, came from the lowest order of worker, those employed in housework and hotels; and the next largest was found among seamstresses, employees of shirt-factories, and cloak-makers, all of these industries in which under pay is proverbial. The great majority, receiving not more than five dollars a week, earn it by seldom less than ten hours a day of hard labor, and not only live on the sum, but assist friends, contribute to general household expenses, dress so as to appear fairly well, and have learned every art of doing without. More than this, since the deepening interest in their lives, and the formation of working-girls' clubs and societies of many orders, they contribute from this scanty sum enough to rent meeting-rooms, pay for instruction in many classes, and provide a relief fund for sick and disabled members.

This is the summary of conditions as a whole, and we pass now to the specific evils and abuses in trades and general industries.

XI.

SPECIFIC EVILS AND ABUSES IN FACTORY LIFE AND IN GENERAL TRADES.

"Has civilization civilized?" is the involuntary question, as one by one the fearful conditions hedging about workers on either side of the sea become apparent. At once, in any specific investigation, we face abuses for which the system of production rather than the employer is often responsible, and for which science has as yet found either none or but a partial remedy. Alike in England and on the Continent work and torture become synonyms, and flesh and blood the cheapest of all nineteenth-century products. The best factory system swarms with problems yet unsolved; the worst, as it may be found in many a remote district of the Continent and even in England itself, is appalling in both daily fact and final result. It would seem at times as if the workshop meant only a form of preparation for the hospital, the workhouse, and the prison, since the workers therein become inoculated with trade diseases, mutilated by trade appliances, and corrupted by trade associates, till no healthy fibre, mental, moral, or physical, remains.

In the nail and chain making districts of England, Sundays are often abolished where these furnaces flame, and such rest as can be stolen comes on the cinder-heaps. But these workers are few compared with the myriads who must battle with the most insidious and most potent of enemies,—the dust of modern manufacture. There is dust of heckling flax, with an average of only fourteen years of work for the strongest; dust of emery powder, that has been known to destroy in a month; dust of pottery and sand and flint, so penetrating that the medical returns give cases of "stone" for new-born babes; dust of rags foul with dirt and breeding fever in the picker; dust of wools from diseased animals, striking down the sorter. Wood, coal, flour, each has its own, penetrating where it can never be dislodged; and a less tangible enemy lurks in poisonous paints for flowers or wall-paper, and in white lead, the foundation of other paints,—blotching the skin of children, and ending for many in blindness, paralysis, and hideous sores.

This is one form; and side by side with it comes another, dealt with here and there, but as a rule ignored,—vapors as deadly as dust; vapors of muriatic acid from pickling tins; of choking chlorine from bleaching-rooms; of gas and phosphorus, which even now, where strongest preventives are used, still pull away both teeth and jaws from many a worker in match-factories; while acids used in cleaning, bleaching-powders, and many an industry where women and children chiefly are employed, eat into hands and clothing, and make each hour a torture.

With the countless forms of machinery for stamping and rolling and cutting and sawing, there is yet, in spite of all the safeguards the law compels, the saying still heard in these shops: "It takes three fingers to make a stamper." Carelessness often; but where two must work together, as is necessary in tending many of these machines, the partner's inattention is often responsible, and mutilation comes through no fault of one's own. Add to all these the suffering of little children taught lace-making at four, sewing on buttons or picking threads far into the night, and driven through the long hours that they may add sixpence to the week's wage, and we have a hint of the grewsome catalogue of the human woe born of human need and human greed.

For the United States there is a steadily lessening proportion of these evils, and we shall deal chiefly with those found in existence by the respective bureaus of labor at the time when their investigations were made. Private and public investigation made before their organization had brought to light in Connecticut, and at many points in New England, gross abuses both in child labor and that of woman and girl workers. It is sufficient, however, for our purpose to refer the reader to the mention of these contained in the first report of the Massachusetts Bureau of Labor, as well as to Dr. Richard T. Ely's "History of the Labor Movement in America," and to pass at once to the facts contained in the fifteenth report from Massachusetts.

The ventilation of factories and of workrooms in general is one of the first points considered. Naturally, facts of this order would be found in the testimony only of the more intelligent. Where factories are new and built expressly for their own purposes, ventilation is considered, and in many is excellent. But in smaller ones and in many industries the structures used were not intended for this purpose. Closely built buildings shut off both light and air, which must come wholly from above, thus preventing circulation, and producing an effect both depressing and wearing. The agents in a number of cases found employees packed "like sardines in a box;" thirty-five persons, for example, in a small attic without ventilation of any kind. Some were in very low-studded rooms, with no ventilation save from windows, causing bad draughts and much sickness, and others in basements where dampness was added to cold and bad air.

In many cases the nature of the trade compelled closed windows, and no provision was made for ventilation in any other way. In one case girls were working in "little pens all shelved over, without sufficient light or air, windows not being open, for fear of cooling wax thread used on sewing-machines."[41]

For a large proportion of the workrooms visited or reported upon was a condition ranging from dirty to filthy. In some where men and women were employed together in tailoring, the report reads:

"Their shop is filthy and unfit to work in. There are no conveniences for women; and men and women use the same closets, wash-basins, and drinking-cups, etc."[42] In another a water-closet in the centre of the room filled it with a sickening stench; yet forty hands were at work here, and there are many cases in which the location of these closets and the neglect of proper disinfectants make not only work-rooms but factories breeding-grounds of disease.

Lack of ventilation in almost all industries is the first evil, and one of the most insidious. Other points affecting health are found in the nature of certain of the trades and the conditions under which they must be carried on. Feather-sorters, fur-workers, cotton-sorters, all workers on any material that gives off dust, are subject to lung and bronchial troubles. In soap-factories the girls' hands are eaten by the caustic soda, and by the end of the day the fingers are often raw and bleeding. In making buttons, pins, and other manufactures of this nature, there is always liability of getting the fingers jammed or caught. For the first three times the wounds are dressed without charge. After that the person injured must pay expenses. In these and many other trades work must be so closely watched that it brings on weakness of the eyes, so that many girls are under treatment for this.

In bakeries the girls stand from ten to sixteen hours a day, and break down after a short time. Boots and shoes oblige being on the feet all day; and this is the case for saleswomen, cash-girls, and all factory-workers. In type-founderies the air is always filled with a fine dust produced by rubbing, and the girls employed have no color in their faces. In paper-box making constant standing brings on the same difficulties found among all workers who stand all day; and they complain also of the poison often resulting from the coloring matter used in making the boxes. In book-binderies, brush-manufactories, etc., the work soon breaks down the girls.

In the clothing-business, where the running of heavy sewing-machines is done by foot-power, there is a fruitful source of disease; and even where steam is used, the work is exhausting, and soon produces weakness and various difficulties.

In food preparations girls who clean and pack fish get blistered hands and fingers from the saltpetre employed by the fishermen.

Others in "working-stalls" stand in cold water all day, and have the hands in cold water; and in laundries, confectionery establishments, etc., excessive heat and standing in steam make workers especially liable to throat and lung diseases, as well as those induced by continuous standing.

Straw goods produce a fine dust, and cause a constant hacking among the girls at work upon them; and the acids used in setting the colors often produce "acid sores" upon the ends of the fingers.

In match-factories, as already mentioned, even with the usual precautions, necrosis often attacks the worker, and the jaw is eaten away. Sores, ulcerations, and suffering of many orders are the portion of workers in chemicals. In many cases a little expenditure on the part of the employer would prevent this; but unless brought up by an inspector, no precautions are taken.

The question of seats for saleswomen comes up periodically, has been at some points legislated upon, and is in most stores ignored or evaded. "The girls look better,—more as if they were ready for work," is the word of one employer, who frankly admitted that he did not mean they should sit; and this is the opinion acted upon by most. Insufficient time for meals is a universal complaint; and nine times out of ten, the conveniences provided are insufficient for the numbers who must use them, and thus throw off offensive and dangerous effluvia.

It is one of the worst evils in shop life, not only for Massachusetts, but for the entire United States, that in all large stores, where fixed rules must necessarily be adopted, girls are forced to ask men for permission to go to closets, and often must run the gauntlet of men and boys. All physicians who treat this class testify to the fact that many become seriously diseased as the result of unwillingness to subject themselves to this ordeal.

One of the ablest factory-inspectors in this country, or indeed in any country, Mrs. Fanny B. Ames of Boston, reports this as one of the least regarded points in a large proportion of the factories and manufacturing establishments visited, but adds that it arises often from pure ignorance and carelessness, and is remedied as soon as attention is called to it.

Taking up the other New England reports in which reference to these evils is found, the testimony is the same. Law is often evaded or wholly set aside, — at times through carelessness, at others wilfully. The most exhaustive treatment of this subject in all its bearings is found in the report of the New Jersey Bureau of Labor for 1889, the larger portion of it being devoted to the fullest consideration of the hygiene of occupation, the diseases peculiar to special trades, and general sanitary condition and methods of working, not only in "dangerous, unhealthy, or noxious trades," but in all. Commissioner Bishop, from whose report quotations have already been made (p. 197), gives many instances of working under fearful conditions, absolutely destructive to health and often to morals; and the report may be regarded as one of the most authoritative words yet spoken in this direction.

The Factory Inspection Law for the State of New York, in detail much the same as that of Massachusetts, is sufficiently full and explicit to secure to all workers better conditions than any as yet attained save in isolated cases. There is, however, constant violation of its most vital points; and this must remain true for all States, until the number of inspectors is made in some degree adequate to the demand. At present they are not only seriously overworked, but find it impossible to cover the required ground. The law which stands at present as the demand to be made by all factory-workers and all interested in intelligent legislation, will be found in the Appendix.

Destructive to health and morals as are often the factories and workshops in which women must work, they play far less part in their lives than the homes afforded by the great cities, where the poor herd in quarters, — at their best only tolerable shelters, at their worst unfit for man or beast. It is the tenement-house question that in these words presents itself for consideration, and that makes part of the general problem. Taking New York as illustrative of some of the worst forms of over-crowding, though Boston and Chicago are not far behind, we turn to the work of one of the closest and most competent of observers, Dr. Annie S. Daniel, for many years physician in charge of out-practice for the New York Infirmary for Women and Children. The report of this practice for 1891 includes a series of facts bearing vitally on every phase of woman's labor.

Known as an expert in these directions, her testimony was called for in the examination of 1893 into the sweating-system of New York, made by a congressional committee and now on record in a report to be had on application to the New York Congressmen at Washington.[43] For years she has watched the effects of child-labor, taking hundreds of measurements of special cases, and studying the effects of the life mothers and children alike were compelled to live. "The medical problems," she writes, "which present themselves to the physician are so closely connected with the social problems that it is impossible to study one alone. The people are sick because of insufficient food and clothing and unsanitary surroundings, and these conditions exist because the people are poor. They are often poor *because they have no work*." At another point, commenting on drinking among the poor, she writes: "Drinking among the women is increasing. In the majority of cases we have studied, it has been the effect of poverty, not the cause."

In the region between Houston Street and Canal Street, known now to be the most thickly populated portion of the inhabited globe, every house is a factory; that is, some form of manufacture is going on in every room. The average family of five adds to itself from two to ten more, often a sewing-machine to each person; and from six or seven in the morning till far into the night work goes on,—usually the manufacture of clothing. Here contagious diseases pass from one to another. Here babies are born and babies die, the work never pausing save for death and hardly for that. In one of these homes Dr. Daniel found a family of five making cigars, the mother included. "Two of the children were ill of diphtheria. Both parents attended to these children; they would syringe the nose of each child, and without washing their hands return to their cigars. We have repeatedly observed the same thing when the work was manufacturing clothing and undergarments to be bought as well by the rich as by the poor. Hand-sewed shoes, made for a fashionable Broadway shoe-store, were sewed at home by a man in whose family were three children sick with scarlet-fever. And such instances are common. Only death or lack of work closes tenement-house manufactories ... When we consider that stopping this work means no food and no roof over their heads, the fact that the disease may be carried by their work cannot be expected to impress the people."

Farther on in the report, she adds: "The people can neither be moral nor healthy until they have decent homes." Yet the present wage-rate makes decent homes impossible; and though Brooklyn and Boston have a few model tenement-houses, New York has none, the experiment of making over in part a few old ones hardly counting save in intention. Into these homes respectable, ambitious, hard-working girls and women are compelled to go. That they live decent lives speaks worlds for the intrinsic goodness and purity of nature which in the midst of conditions intolerable to every sense still preserves these characteristics. That they must live in such surroundings is one of the deepest disgraces of civilization.

As to wages, concerning which there seems to be a general opinion that steady rise has gone on, we find Dr. Daniel giving the rates for many years. She writes: —

> "Wages have steadily decreased. Among the women who earned the whole or part of the income, finishing pantaloons was the most common occupation. For this work, in 1881, they received ten to fifteen cents a pair; for the same work in 1891, three to five, at the most ten cents a pair. The women doing this work claim that wages are reduced because of the influx of Italian women, but few Italian women do the poor quality of trousers. While we are glad to note some excellent sanitary changes in the tenement-house construction, the people we believe to be just as poor, just as overcrowded and wretched to-day, as in 1881 and 1853, the only difference being that there are a greater number of people who are poor now."

These statements apply in great part to unskilled labor; but there is always in these houses a large proportion of skilled labor disabled by sickness or other causes and out of work for the time being. The wage at best for skilled labor is given by the Labor Commissioner as $5.29. Let any one study the possibilities of this sum per week, and the wonder will arise, not why living is not easier, but how it goes on at all.

Specific evils speak for themselves, and are gradually being eliminated. They are before the eyes, and the least experienced student may gauge their bearing and judge their effects. But wider-reaching than any or all the worst abuses of the worst trades is the wrong done to the child and to family life as a whole, by the continuous labor of married women in factories, or at any occupation which demands, for ten hours or more a day, unremitting toil. At all points where scientific observation has been made the expert lifts up a warning voice. It is the future of the race that is in question. Child labor, while not entering directly into our present examination, is, as has already been said, inextricably bound up with the question of woman's work and wages. The two must be studied together; and for our own country there are already admirable monographs on this subject,[44] two authoritative ones coming from the American Economic Association, and one hardly less so from a close and keen observer whose scientific training gives her equal right to form conclusions.[45]

A dispassionate observer, Mr. W. Stanley Jevons, whose conclusions are founded on long investigation and deduction, years ago wrote words which he has at various times emphasized and repeated, and which sum up the evils to which the infancy of the children of overworked mothers is subject, as well as the consequences to the State in which they are born, and which faces the results of the system which produces them. He writes as follows:—

> "We can help evolution by the aid of its own highest and latest product,—science. When all the teaching of medical and social science lead us to look upon the absence of the mother from the home as the cause of the gravest possible evils, can we be warranted in standing passively by, allowing this evil to work itself out to the bitter end, by the process of natural selection? Something might perhaps be said in favor of the present apathetic mode of viewing this question, if natural selection were really securing the survival of the fittest, so that only the weakly babes were killed off, and the strong ones well brought up. But it is much to be feared that no infants ever really recover from the

test of virtual starvation to which they are so ruthlessly exposed. The vital powers are irreparably crippled, and the infant grows up a stunted, miserable specimen of humanity, the prey to every physical and moral evil."[46]

It is hardly necessary to go on specifying special violations of sanitary law or special illustrative cases. The Report of the New York Bureau of Labor for 1885 is a magazine of such cases, — a summary of all the horrors that the worst conditions can include. Aside from the revolting pictures of the life lived from day to day by the workers themselves, it gives in detail case after case of rapacity and overreaching on the part of the employers; and parallel ones may be found in every labor report which has touched upon the subject.

In New York a "Working Woman's Protective Union," formed more than twenty-five years ago, has done unceasing work in settling disputed claims and collecting wages unjustly withheld. No case is entered on their books which has not been examined by their lawyer, and thus only well grounded complaints find record; but with even these precautions the records show nearly fifty thousand adjudicated since they began work. Many cities have special committees, in the organized charities, who seek to cover the same ground, but who find it impossible to do all that is required. From East and West alike, complaints are practically the same. It is not only women in trades, but those in domestic service, who are recorded as suffering every form of oppression and injustice. Colorado and California, Kansas and Wisconsin, speak the same word. With varying industries wrongs vary, but the general summary is the same.

The system of fines, while on general principles often just, has been used by unscrupulous employers to such a degree as to bring the week's wages down a third or even half. It is impossible to give illustrative instances in detail; but all who deal with girls, in clubs and elsewhere, report that the system requires modification.

On the side of the employers, and as bearing also on the evils which are most marked among women workers, we may quote from the Government Report, "Working Women in Large Cities": —

"Actual ill-treatment by employers seems to be infrequent.... Foreigners are often found to be more considerate of their help than native-born men, and the kindest proprietor in the world is a Jew of the better class. In some shops week-workers are locked out for the half-day if late, or docked for every minute of time lost, an extra fine being often added. Piece workers have great freedom as to hours, and employers complain much of tardiness and absenteeism. The mere existence of health and labor laws insures privileges formerly unheard of; half-holidays in summer, vacation with pay, and shorter hours are becoming every year more frequent, better workshops are constructed, and more comfortable accommodations are being furnished."

This is most certainly true, but more light shows the shadows even more clearly; and the fact remains that every force must be brought to bear, to remedy the evils depicted in the reports of the bureaus quoted here.

The general conditions of working-women in New York retail stores were reported upon, in 1890, by a committee from the Working-Woman's Society, at 27 Clinton Place, New York. The report was read at a mass meeting held at Chickering Hall, May 6, 1890; and its statements represent general conditions in all the large cities of the United States. It is impossible to give more than the principal points of the report; but readers can obtain it on application to the Secretary of the Association.[47] These are as follows: —

Hours are often excessive, and employees are not paid for overtime. Many stores give no half-holiday, and keep open on Saturdays till ten and eleven o'clock in the evening, and at the holiday season do this for three or four weeks nightly.

Sanitary conditions are usually bad, and include bad ventilation, unsanitary arrangements, and indifference to the considerations of decency. Toilet arrangements in many stores are horrible, and closets for male and female are often side by side, with only slight partition between. One hand-basin and towel serve for all. Often water for drink can be obtained only from the attic.

Numbers of children under age are employed for excessive hours, and at work far beyond their strength, an investigation having shown that over one hundred thousand children under the legal age of fourteen were at work in factories, workshops, and stores.

Service for a number of years often meets with no consideration, but is regarded as a reason for dismissal. It is the rule in some stores to keep no one over five years, lest they come to feel that they have some claim on the firm; and when a saleswoman is dismissed from one house, she finds it almost impossible to obtain employment in another.

The wages are reduced by excessive fines, employers placing a value upon time lost that is not given to services rendered. The fines run from five to thirty cents for a few minutes' tardiness. In some stores the fines are divided at the end of the year between the time-keeper and the superintendent, and there is thus every temptation to injustice.

The report concludes: —

> "We find that, through low wages, long hours, unwholesome sanitary conditions, and the discouraging effect of excessive fines, not only is the physical condition injured, but the tendency is to injure the moral well-being. It is simply impossible for a woman to live without assistance on the low salary a saleswoman earns, without depriving herself of real necessities."

These were the conditions which, in 1889, led to the formation of the little society which, though limited in numbers, has done admirable and efficient work, its latest effort being to secure from the Assembly at Albany a bill making inspection of stores and shops as obligatory as that of factories.

It was through the concerted effort of its members that the Factory Inspection Act became a law, though not without violent opposition. The bill originated in the Working-Woman's Society, was drawn up there, sent to Albany by its delegates, and passed without the aid of money.

There are eleven thousand factories in New York State, and only one inspector to investigate their condition; while in England, scarce larger in territory, forty-one inspectors are appointed by the Government.

The Andrus bill, adding to the power of factory inspectors, raising the working age of children to fourteen years, and prohibiting night work for girls under twenty-one and boys under eighteen, was sent with the Factory Bill to the Central Labor Union, and the women were largely instrumental in obtaining the passage of the measure.

Why such determined opposition still meets every attempt to bring about the same inspection for mercantile establishments cannot be determined; but thus far, though admitted to be necessary, the act has at each reading been laid upon the table. Another effort will be made in the coming winter of 1893-94.

In spite, however, of much agitation of all phases of woman's work, it is only some wrong as startling as that involved in the sweating-system that seems able to arouse more than a temporary interest. One of the most able and experienced women inspectors of the United States Bureau of Labor, Miss de Grafenried, has lately written: —

> "It is an open question whether woman's pay is not falling, cost and standards of living considered. Could partly supported labor and children be eliminated, shop employees would get higher rates. Still there are other economic anomalies that affect women's wages. 'Wholesalers' and manufacturers shut up their factories and 'give out' everything — umbrellas, coats, hair-wigs, and shrouds — to be made, — they know not in what den, or wrung they care not from what misery ... Again, wages are depressed by over-stimulating piece-work; and its unscrupulous use by proprietors who hesitate to confess to paying women only $3 or $4 a week, yet who scale prices so that only experts can earn that sum. Many employers cut rates as soon as, by desperate exertions, operatives clear

$5 a week. Then, underbidding from the unem-
ployed is a fruitful source of low wages. Massachusetts has 20 per cent of her workers unemployed."

These conditions, while varying as to numbers, are practically the same for the work of women in all parts of the United States, and are matters of increasing perplexity and sorrow to every searcher into these problems. At its best, woman's work in industries is intermittent, since it is only textile work that continues the year round; dress and cloak making, shoe and umbrella making, fur-sewing and millinery, have specific seasons, in the intervals between which the worker waits and starves, or, if too desperate, goes upon the streets, driven there by the wretched competitive system, the evils of which increase in direct ratio to the longing for speedy wealth. In short, matters are at that point where only radical change of methods can better the situation, even the most conservative observer, relying most thoroughly upon evolution, feeling something more than evolution must work if justice is to have place in the present social scheme.

It is at this point that some consideration of domestic service naturally presents itself. Though regarded often as no part of the labor question, there can be no other head under which to range it, since the last census gives over a million persons engaged in this occupation, the lowest rough estimate of wages being $160,000,000 and the support included forming a sum at least as large. It is through the hands of the domestic servant that a large part of the finished products of other forms of labor must pass, and the economic aspects of the question grow in importance with every year of the changing conditions of American life. In no other occupation is a just consideration of the points involved so difficult a task, since the mistress who faces the incompetence, insubordination, and all the other trials involved in the relation, suffers too keenly from the sense of individual wrong to treat the matter in the large. Till it is so treated, however, understanding for both sides is impossible, and to bring about such understanding is the first necessity for all.

From the employer's standpoint the advantages to be stated are as follows: First and most obvious is the fact that wages are not only relatively but absolutely high; for aside from the actual cash there are also board, lodging, fuel, light, and laundry, all of which the worker in trades must provide for herself. There is no capital required, as for type-writer, sewing-machine, or any appliances for work, nor is the girl forced to expend anything in preparation, since under the present system housekeepers take her untrained fresh from Castle Garden, and willingly give the needed instruction, at the same time paying the same wage as that given to competent service. Professor Lucy Salmon, of Vassar, who has devoted much time to this subject, reports that, on examination of testimony from three thousand employees, it is found that on a wage of $3.25 a week it is possible to save annually nearly $150 "in an occupation involving no outlay, no investment of capital, and few or no personal expenses." The wages received are relatively higher than those of other occupations; for in Professor Salmon's comparison of wages received by three thousand country and the same number of city employees it was found that of six thousand teachers in the public schools the average salary actually paid is less than that paid to the average cook in a large city.

The second advantage lies in the healthfulness of the work, which includes not only regularity but variety; the third, that a home, at least in all externals, is insured; the fourth, that a training which makes the worker more fit for married life is certain; and a fifth, that the work is congenial and easy for those whose tastes lie in this direction.

These are the facts that are constantly urged upon the army of under-paid, half-starving needlewomen in our great cities, and no less upon another army of girls in shops and factories, who are implored to consider the advantages of domestic service and to give up their unnecessary battle with the limitations hedging in every other form of labor. Astonishment that the girls prefer the factory and shop is unending, nor is it regarded as possible that substantial reason may and must exist for such choice. As a means of arriving at some solution of the problem, some six hundred employees of every order were interviewed, under circumstances which made their replies perfectly free and full; and the results tallied exactly with others obtained by an inquiry in the Philadelphia Working-

Woman's Guild, a society then representing seventy-two distinct occupations.

A report of this inquiry was made by Mrs. Eliza S. Turner, the President of the Guild, and is given as the most suggestive view of the whole subject yet secured. She writes as follows: —

> "Why do not intelligent, refined girls more frequently choose house service as a support?" The replies here given are as nearly as possible *verbatim*:
>
> 1. Loss of freedom. This is as dear to women as to men, although we don't get so much of it. The day of a saleswoman or a factory hand may be long, but when it is done she is her own mistress; but in service, except when she is actually out of the house, she has no hour, no minute, when her soul is her own.
>
> 2. Hurts to self-respect. One thing that makes housework unpleasant—chamber-work, for instance, and waiting on table—is that it is a kind of personal service, one human being waiting on another. The very thing you would do without a thought in your own home for your own family seems menial when it is demanded by a stranger.
>
> 3. The very words, "service" and "servant," are hateful. It is all well enough to talk about service being divine, but that is not the way the world looks at it.
>
> 4. Say that a young woman well brought up undertakes to do chamber-work; she is obliged to associate with the other girls, no matter how uncongenial they may be, what may be their language or personal habits or table manners. If she tries to keep to herself, the rest think she is taking airs, and combine to make her life unbearable.
>
> 5. Or say she takes a place for general housework; to be alone in the midst of others is crush-

ing, — quite different from being alone in one's own lodgings.

6. I suppose a soldier doesn't mind being ordered around by his captain; but in a family the mistress and maid are so mixed up that it is much harder to keep the lines from tangling. It takes a very superior person, on both sides, to do it.

7. I knew an educated woman — a lady — who tried it as a sort of upper housemaid. The work was easy, the pay good, and she never had a harsh word; but they just seemed unconscious of her existence. She said the gentlemen of the house, father and son, would come in and stand before her to have her take their umbrellas or help them off with their coats, and sometimes without speaking to her or even looking at her. There was something so humiliating about it that she couldn't stand it, but went back to slop shop sewing.

8. Many mistresses have no standard of the amount of work a girl ought to do. They know nothing about housework themselves. If a girl is deliberate and saves herself, they call her slow; if she is ambitious, and gets her work done early, and they see her sitting down in working-hours, they conclude that she is not earning her wages, and hunt up some extra job for her. No matter if you can't find anything undone, if she is found sitting about she *must* be lazy.

9. Some employers think that after the more violent work is done, it is only a rest for the girl to look after the child awhile. They don't seem to realize that if the mother finds it such a relief to get rid of her own child for an hour or so, it is likely to be still less interesting to take care of somebody else's child.

10. Many people think the position of a child's nurse is very light work indeed, — mostly just sit-

ting around; so they don't hesitate to give her the care of one or two children all day, not even arranging for her to get her meals without the oversight of them; and then most likely put the baby to sleep with her at night. Any one minute of such a day may not be heavy, but to have it for twenty-four hours is enough to wear out the strongest human being ever made.

11. I knew a school-teacher who thought more active occupation would better suit her health; she took a place as child's nurse. She loved children, and found no objection to the work; but soon the employer concluded to put her in a *bonne's* cap and apron. My friend would have worn and liked a nurse's uniform, but she objected to a family livery. On this question they parted; and her employer hired an uncouth, ignorant woman to be her child's companion and to give it its first impressions.

12. In most houses, however elegant, the girls have no home privacy; they must sleep, not only in the same room, but most frequently in the same bed; it is rarely thought necessary to make that room pleasant or even warm for them to dress by or to sit in to do their own sewing. The little tastes and notions of each member of the family, down to the youngest, are provided for; but a "girl" is not supposed to have any. She is just a "girl," as a gridiron is a gridiron, an article bought for the convenience of the family. If she suits, use her till she is worn out and then throw her away.

13. To go into house service, even from the most wretched slop or factory work, is to lose caste in our own world; it may be a very narrow world, but it is all to us. A saleswoman or cashier or teacher is ashamed to associate with servants.

14. The very words, "No followers," would keep us out of such occupation. No self-respecting young woman is going to put herself in a position where she is not allowed to entertain her friends, both male and female; nor where, if allowed, the only place thought fit for them is the kitchen.

Now, the above is not theory, but testimony, taken by the present writer from the lips of intelligent working-girls, many of whom would be better off at housework than at their present occupations, except for the objections. And from a consideration thereof results this query: Given a certain number of young women of a class superior to the imported, willing to take service under the following conditions, how many housekeepers would agree to the conditions? —

1. The heaviest work, as washing, carrying coal, scrubbing pavements, and the like, to be provided for, if this be asked, with consequent deduction in wages.

2. In families, where practicable, certain hours of absolute freedom while in the house, especially with the child's nurse.

3. Such a way of speaking, both to and of your house help, as testifies to the world that you really do consider housework as respectable as other occupations.

4. A well-warmed, well-furnished room, with separate beds when desired; and the use of a decent place and appointments at meals.

5. The privilege of seeing friends, whether male or female; of a better part of the house than the kitchen in which to receive them; and security from espionage during their visits, — this accompanied by proper restrictions as to evening hours,

and under the condition that the work is not neglected.

6. No livery, if objected to.

Turning from this informal examination of the subject to the few labor reports which have taken up the matter, it becomes plain that domestic service is in many points more undesirable than any other occupation open to women. The Labor Commissioner of Minnesota reports, while stating all the advantages of the domestic servant over the general worker, that "only a fifth of those who employ them are fit to deal with any worker, injustice and oppression characterizing their methods." Figures and detailed statements bear him out in this conclusion. The Colorado Commissioner gives even more details, and comes to the same conclusion; and though other reports do not take up the subject in detail, their indications are the same.

The first general and rational presentation of the subject in all its bearings, both for employed and employer, has lately been made during the Woman's Congress at Chicago, May, 1893, in which the Domestic Science section discussed every phase of wrongs and remedies.[48] The latter sum up in the formation of bureaus of employment in every large city, fixed rates, and full preparatory training. A keen observer of social facts has stated: The intelligence offices of New York alone receive from servants yearly over three million dollars, and are notoriously inefficient. This, or even half of it, would provide a great centre with training-schools, lodgings for all who needed them, and a system by which fixed rates were made according to the grade of efficiency of the worker. Till household service comes under the laws determining value, as well as hours and all other points involved in the wage for a working-day, it will remain in the disorganized and hopeless state which at present baffles the housekeeper, and deters self-respecting women and girls from undertaking it. To bring about some such organization as that suggested will most quickly accomplish this; and there seems already hope that the time is not distant when every city will have its agency corresponding to the great Bourse du Travail in Paris, but even more comprehensive in scope. Co-operation within certain limited degrees, so that private home life will not be infringed upon, must necessarily make part of such a scheme, and has already been tried with success at various points in the West; but details can hardly be given here. It is sufficient to add that with such new basis for this form of occupation the "servant question" will cease to be a terror, and the most natural occupation for women will have countless recruits from ranks now closed against it.

FOOTNOTES:

[41] Fifteenth Annual Report of the Massachusetts Bureau of Labor, p. 68.

[42] Ibid.

[43] House of Representatives Report No. 2309: Report of the Committee on Manufactures on the Sweating-System, House of Representatives, January, 1893.

[44] Child Labor. By William F. Willoughby, A.B. Child Labor. By Miss Clare de Grafenried, Publications of the American Economic Association, vol. v. no. 2.

[45] Our Toiling Children. By Florence Kelley, W.C.T.U. Publishing Association, Chicago.

[46] Married Women in Factories. By W. Stanley Jevons, Contemporary Review, vol. xli. pp. 37-53.

[47] Miss Alice Woodbridge, Secretary of the Working-Woman's Society, 27 Clinton Place, New York.

[48] The association then formed, and from which much is hoped, made the following summary of its objects: —

> "The objects of this Association shall be: 1. To awaken the public mind to the importance of establishing a Bureau of Information where there can be an exchange of wants and needs between employer and employed in every department of home and social life. 2. To promote among members of the Association a more scientific knowledge of the economic value of various foods and fuels; a more intelligent understanding of correct plumbing and drainage in our homes, as well as need for pure water and good light in a sanitarily built house. 3. To secure skilled labor in every department of women's work in our homes, — not only to demand better trained cooks and waitresses, but to consider the importance of meeting the increasing demand

for those competent to do plain sewing and mend-
ing."

XII.

REMEDIES AND SUGGESTIONS.

The student of social problems who faces the misery of the lowest
order of worker, and the sharp privation endured by many even of
the better class, is apt, in the first fever of amazement and indignation, to feel that some instant force must be brought to bear, and
justice secured, though the heavens fall. It is this sense of the struggle of humanity out of which have been born Utopias of every order, from the "Republic" of Plato to the dream in "Looking Backward." Not one of these can be spared; and that they exist and find a
following larger and larger, is the surest evidence of the soul at the
bottom of each. But for those who take the question as a whole, who
see how slow has been the process of evolution, and how impossible it is to hasten one step of the unfolding that humankind is still to
know, it is the ethical side that comes uppermost, and that first demands consideration.

Taking the mass of the lowest order of workers at all points, the
first aim of any effort intended for their benefit is to disentangle the
individual from the mass. It is not charity that is to do this. "Homes"
of every variety open their doors; but in all of them still lurks the
suspicion of charity; and even when this has no active formulation
in the worker's mind, there is still the underlying sense of the essential injustice of withholding with one hand just pay, and with the
other proffering a substitute, in a charity which is to reflect credit on
the giver and demand gratitude from the receiver. Here and there
this is recognized, and within a short time has been emphasized by
a woman whose name is associated with the work of organized
charities throughout the country,—Mrs. Josephine Shaw Lowell. It
is doubtful if there is any woman in the country better fitted, by
long experience and almost matchless common-sense, to speak au-
thoritatively. She writes:—

> "So far from assuming that the well-to-do por-
> tion of society have discharged all their obligations
> to men and God by supporting charitable institu-
> tions, I regard just this expenditure as one of the
> prime causes of the suffering and crime that exist
> in our midst.... I am inclined, in general, to look
> upon what is called charity as the insult added to
> the injury done to the mass of the people, by insuf-
> ficient payment for work."

Just pay, then, heads the list of remedies. The difficulty of fixing this is necessarily enormous, nor can it come at once; since education for not only the employer but the public as a whole is demanded. To bring this about is a slow process. It is a transition period in which we live. Material conditions born of phenomenal material progress have deadened the sense as to what constitutes real progress; and the working-woman of to-day contends not only with visible but invisible obstacles, the nature of which we are but just beginning to discern. Twenty years ago M. Paul Leroy-Beaulieu wrote of women wage-earners: —

> "From the economic point of view, woman, who
> has next to no material force, and whose arms are
> advantageously replaced by the least machine, can
> have useful place and obtain a fair remuneration
> only by the development of the best qualities of
> her intelligence. It is the inexorable law of our civi-
> lization, — the principle and formula even of social
> progress, — that mechanical engines are to perform
> every operation of human labor which does not
> proceed directly from the mind. The hand of man
> is each day deprived of a portion of its original
> task; but this general gain is a loss for the particu-
> lar, and for the classes whose only instrument of
> labor is a pair of feeble arms."

Take the fact here stated, and add to it all that is implied in modern competitive conditions, and we see the true nature of the task that awaits us. To do away with this competition would not accomplish the end desired. To guide it and bring it into intelligent lines is part of the general education. Profit-sharing is an indispensable portion of the justice to be done; and this, too, implies education for both sides, and would go far toward lessening burdens. We cannot abolish the factory, but hours can be shortened; the labor of married women with young children forbidden, as well as that of children below a fixed age. Industrial education will prevent the possibility of another generation owning so many incompetent and untrained workers, and technical schools in general are already raising the standard and helping to secure the same end.

Our present methods mean waste in every direction, and trusts and syndicates have already demonstrated how much may be saved to the producer if intelligent combination can be brought about. Competition can never wholly be set aside, since within reasonable limits it is the spur of invention and a part of evolution itself. But if wise co-operation be once adopted, the enormous friction and waste of present methods ceases,—the waste of human life as well as of material.

One cheering token of progress is the increased discussion as to methods of training and the necessity of organization among women themselves. Ten years ago only a voice here and there suggested the need of either. In 1885, at the meeting of the British Association for the Advancement of Science, Miss Sarah Harland, lecturer on Mathematics at Newnham College, insisted that educated gentlewomen must have larger opportunity for paying work. The three qualifications in all work she stated to be: (1) Organization on a large scale; (2) Permanency; (3) Giving returns that will enable the salaries paid to compete with those of teachers.

She regarded dressmaking as the trade which could most readily organize and meet the other conditions specified, and millinery as the trade which would come next. Until such organization and its results have gradually altered present conditions, it will be true for all workers, on both sides of the sea, that not health alone but life itself are continuously endangered by the facts hedging about all labor. Dr. Stevens, the head of St. Luke's Insane Asylum in London, in a paper read before the Social Science Association, said:—

> "It may be stated with great confidence that a
> prolific cause for the rapid and extensive increase

of insanity in this country is to be found in the unceasing toil and anxiety to which the working-classes are subjected, this cause developing the disease in the existing generation, or, what is quite as frequently the case, transmitting to the offspring idiocy, insanity, or some imperfectly developed sensorium or nervous system. The agitated, over-worked, and harassed parent is not in a condition to transmit a healthy brain to his child."[49]

Accepted as true in 1857, the words are not less so to-day, when cheap labor swarms, and the unemployed number their millions.

How best to combine and to what ends, is the lesson taught in every form of the new movement for organization among women. To learn how to work together and what power lies in combination, has been the lesson of all clubs. Among men it has counted as one of the chief educating forces, but for women every circumstance has fostered the distrust of each other which belongs to all undeveloped natures. For the lowest order of worker even, the "Working-Woman's Journal," published in London and the organ of the Working-Woman's Protective Union, has for the last year recorded, from month to month, the gradual progress of the idea of combination, and the new hope it has brought to all who have gone into trades unions.

With us there has been equal need and equal ignorance of all that such combinations have to give. They mean arbitration rather than strikes, and the compelling of ignorant and unjust employers to consider the situation from other points of view than their own. They compel also the same attitude from men in the same trades, who often are as strong opponents of a better chance for their associates among women workers in the same branches, as the most prejudiced employer.

Six points are urged by the Working-Woman's Society of New York, all in the lines indicated here. Its purposes and aims, as given in the prospectus, are as follows: —

> 1. To encourage women in the various trades to protect their mutual interests by organization.

2. To use all possible means to enforce the existing laws relating to the protection of women and children in factories and shops, investigating all reported violations of such laws; also to promote, by all suitable means, further legislation in this direction.

3. To work for the abolition of tenement-house manufacture, especially in the cigar and clothing trades.

4. To investigate all reported cases of cruel treatment on the part of employers and their managers to their women and children employees, in withholding money due, in imposing fines, or in docking wages without sufficient reason.

5. To found a labor bureau for the purpose of facilitating the exchanging of labor between city and country, thus relieving the over-crowded occupations now filled by women.

6. To publish a journal in the interests of working-women.

7. To secure equal pay for both sexes for equal work.

These points are the same as those made by the few clubs which have taken up the question of woman's work and wages; but thus far only this society has formulated them definitely. Working-girls' clubs, friendly societies, and guilds are giving to the worker new thoughts and new purposes. The Convention of Working-Girls' Clubs held in New York in April, 1890, showed the wide-reaching influence they had attained, and the new ideals opening before the worker. It showed also with equal force the roused sense of responsibility toward them, and the eager interest and desire for their betterment in all ways. Where they themselves touched upon their needs, there were direct statements in the same line as many already quoted, which called for better pay, better conditions, shorter hours, and fewer fines.

Following the points given above came another presentation, the result of still further and long-continued investigation; and as the methods of the search and its results are practicable for all towns and cities where women are at work, the statement prepared for the Society is given in full: —

"We would call your attention to the condition of the women and children in the large retail houses in this city, — conditions which tend to injure both physically and morally, not only these women and children, but working-women in general. The general idea is that saleswomen are employed from eight A.M. to six P.M., but they are really engaged in the majority of stores for such a time as the firm requires them; which means in the Grand Street stores, until ten, eleven, and twelve o'clock on Saturday night *all the year round*, the Saturday half-holiday not being observed in summer; and in the majority of houses that stock must be arranged after six P.M., the time varying, according to season, from fifteen minutes to five hours, *and this without supper or extra pay*; thus compelling women and children to go long distances late at night, and rendering them liable to insult and immoral influences.

"Excessive fines are imposed in many stores, — fines varying from ten to thirty cents for ten minutes' tardiness in the morning or lunch hour, and for all mistakes. Cases are known of girls who have been fined a full week's pay at the end of the week. In one store the fines amounted to $3,000 in a year, and the sum was divided between the superintendent and timekeeper; and the superintendent was heard to charge the timekeeper with not being strict enough in his duties.

"Bad sanitary conditions, bad ventilation and toilet arrangements are common, and the sanitary laws are not observed. Children under age are employed at work far beyond their strength, often far into the night. The average wages do not exceed $4.50; and in one of our largest stores the average wage is $2.40, in another $2.90. The tendency in all stores is to secure the cheapest help; for this reason school-girls just graduated are much sought for, as they, having homes, can afford to work for less. But a large proportion of the saleswomen either pay board or help support a family; and how can this be done on $4.50 per week? The cheapest board in dark stuffy attics or tenement houses is $3.00, fuel and washing extra; and no woman can pay doctor's bills and maintain a respectable appearance on what remains. How then does she live? There are two ways of answering: The story of a woman who worked in one of our large houses is one way. This woman earned $3.00 per week; she paid $1.50 for her room; her breakfast consisted of a cup of coffee; she had no lunch; she had but one meal a day. Many saleswomen must be in this condition. The other answer is that given by more than one employer, who when saleswomen complain of the low wages offered, reply: 'Oh, well, get yourself a gentleman friend; *most of our girls have them.*' Not long since a member of our society received a letter from a salesman in a certain house which read thus: 'In the name of God cannot something be done for the saleswomen? I am a salesman in — —, and I have walked in disguise at night upon certain streets to be accosted by girls in my own department, — girls whose salaries are so low it was impossible to live upon them." A painter told us that in working in the houses of ill-repute in the vicinity of Twenty-third Street, he was astonished at the number of women whom he recognized as saleswomen in different stores who frequented these houses. But what are they to do? They are women without trade or profession, thrown upon their own resources, obliged to make a good appearance, and unable to do so and yet have sufficient food. We must all concede that virtue and honor in woman are natural, and very few women resort to such ways unless forced to do so; certainly not, when they yet have sufficient pride to wish to maintain the appearance of respectability. If men's wages fall below a certain limit, they become tramps, thieves, and robbers; but woman's wages *have no limit*, since she can always work for less than she can subsist upon, the *paths of shame being open to her*. And the beggarly pittance for which one class of women work becomes the standard of wages for all women, and throws them out upon the world, there to find a sure market. But we do not wish to insinuate, in stating these facts, that the majority of saleswomen resort to evil ways; on the contrary, they are the exception who do so. We know the majority of women prefer to suffer, and do suffer, rather than do so. But can we allow a few to fall? We of the Working-Women's Society believe that we are so far our sisters' keepers that we are responsible for their position.

"We believe that the payment and condition of those who work (through their employers) for us is our affair, and we have no right to remain in an ignorance that involves or may involve their misery. We believe we have no right, having obtained such knowledge, to refrain from seeking to remedy it, and urging all to assist us to do so.

"In this belief we call your attention to the proposed 'Consumers' League,' the members of which shall pledge themselves to deal at those stores where just conditions exist.

"We have gotten together a number of facts which we shall be glad to present to you with our estimate of a fair house, or one which under existing conditions is eligible to admission to a white list."

Preceding this appeal and the public meetings which ensued, came, in 1890, the formation of the Consumers' League, Mrs. Josephine Shaw Lowell its President. Quiet and inconspicuous as its work has been, the best retail mercantile houses in New York have accepted its prospectus as just, and stand now upon the "White List," which numbers all merchants who seek to deal justly and fairly with their employees. "What constitutes a Fair House" expresses all the needs and formulates the most vital demands of the working-woman; and the results already accomplished speak for themselves. As a guide to other workers, it is given here in full: —

STANDARD OF A FAIR HOUSE.

Wages.

A fair house is one in which equal pay is given for work of equal value, irrespective of sex. In the departments where women only are employed, in which the minimum wages are six dollars per week for experienced adult workers, and fall in few instances below eight dollars.

In which wages are paid by the week.

In which fines, if imposed, are paid into a fund for the benefit of the employees.

In which the minimum wages of cash-girls are two dollars per week, with the same conditions regarding weekly payments and fines.

Hours.

A fair house is one in which the hours from eight A.M. to six P.M. (with three quarters of an hour for lunch) constitute the working-day, and a general half-holiday is given on one day of each week during at least two summer months.

In which a vacation of not less than one week is given with pay during the summer season.

In which all over-time is compensated for.

Physical Conditions.

A fair house is one in which work, lunch, and re-tiring rooms are apart from each other, and con-form in all respects to the present sanitary laws.

In which the present law regarding the provid-ing of seats for saleswomen is observed, and the use of seats permitted.

Other Conditions.

A fair house is one in which humane and con-siderate behavior toward employees is the rule.

In which fidelity and length of service meet with the consideration which is their due.

In which no children under fourteen years of age are employed.

Membership.

The condition of membership shall be the ap-proval by signature of the object of the Consumers' League; and all persons shall be eligible for mem-bership excepting such as are engaged in the retail business in this city, either as employer or employ-ee.

The members shall not be bound never to buy at other shops.

The names of the members of the Consumers' League shall not be made public.

Later, one of the ablest workers in this field, Mrs. Florence Kelley, formulated a basis for every society of working-women, as follows:

I. To bring out of the chaos of competition the order of co-operation.

II. To organize all wages-earning women.

III. To disseminate the literature of labor and co-operation.

IV. To institute a label which shall enable the purchaser to discriminate in favor of goods produced under healthful conditions.

V. 1. Abolition of child labor to the age of sixteen.

2. Compulsory education to the age of sixteen.

3. Prohibition of employment of minors more than eight hours daily.

4. Prohibition of employment of minors at dangerous occupations.

5. Appointment of women inspectors, one for every thousand women and children employed.

6. Healthful conditions of work for women and children.

The foregoing to be obtained by legislation.

The following to be obtained by organization: —

1. Equal pay for equal work with men.

2. A minimal rate which will enable the least paid to live upon her earnings.

A little later, the statement which follows, became necessary: —

"Certain abuses exist in the dry-goods houses affecting the well-being of the saleswomen and children employed, which we believe can be remedied. In fact, in different stores some of them have been remedied, which gives us courage to bring these matters to your attention.

"We find the hours are often excessive, and that these women and children are not paid for overtime.

"We find that in many houses the saleswomen work under unwholesome conditions; these comprise bad ventilation, unsanitary toilet arrangements, and an indifference to considerations of decency.

"The wages, which are low, we find are often reduced by excessive fines; that employers place a value on time lost that they fail to give for service rendered.

"We find that numbers of children under age are employed for excessive hours, and at work far beyond their strength.

"We find that long and faithful service does not meet with the consideration that is its due; on the contrary, having served a certain number of years is a reason for dismissal.

"Because of the foregoing low wages, the discouraging result of excessive fines, long hours, and unwholesome sanitary conditions, not only the physical system is injured, but—the result we most deplore, and of which we have incontrovertible proof—the tendency *is to injure the moral well-being*.

"We believe that to call attention to these evils is to go far toward remedying them, and that the power to do this lies largely in the hands of the purchasing classes.

"We think that 'the payment and condition of those who work—through their employers—for us, is our affair, and that we have no right to remain in ignorance of the conditions that involve or may involve their misery.'"

Two points still remain untouched, both of them vital elements in the just working of the social scheme,—profit-sharing, and a board of conciliation and arbitration for the adjustment of all difficulties between employer and employed.

For every detail bearing upon the education bound up in even the attempt at profit-sharing, as well as for the actual and successful results in this direction, the reader is referred to an excellent little monograph on the subject, "Sharing the Profits," by Miss Mary Whiton Calkins, A.M., and for very full and elaborate treatment of the question, to the invaluable volume by N.P. Gilman, "Profit-Sharing between Employer and Employed." In all cases where the experiment has had fair trial, it has resulted in a marked increase of interest in the work itself; an actual lessening of the cost of production, and of general wear and tear, because of this increased interest; and a far more friendly feeling between employer and employed. It is certain that justice requires immediate attention to every phase of this question, and that its adoption is the first step in the right direction.

For the second point, we have as yet in this country only an occasional attempt at arbitration, yet its need becomes more and more apparent with every fresh difficulty in the field of labor. A little volume by Mrs. Josephine Shaw Lowell, at the time of writing,[50] going through the press, who has given much time to a study of the question, contains the latest results of English and French legislation, and of special action in this direction. Any history of the movement as a whole, hardly has place in these pages. It is sufficient to say that the system had practically no consideration till 1850, when the first Board of Arbitration was formed in England, owing its existence to the determined efforts of two men. Mr. Rupert Kettle, lawyer and judge, approached it from the legal side; Mr. Murdella, a manufacturer, and himself sprung from the working-classes, went straight "to the practical and moral end implied by the word 'conciliation,' ... both routes of this noble emulation converging, each affording strength to the common conclusions."

The Nottingham lace manufacture, in which numbers of women and children as well as men are employed, has, for thirty years and more, been governed by a Board of Arbitration, the result being an end of strikes and all difficulties of like nature. If no more were accomplished than the bringing about a better understanding between employer and employed, it would mean much, since mutual suspicion and distrust rule for both. Organization among women, and the sense of mutual dependence given by it, lead naturally to the formation of a board able to judge dispassionately and disinterestedly of the questions naturally arising, many of which, however, are at once dissipated on the adoption of the system of profit-sharing.

The practical steps already taken sum up in the forms just given; and there remains only the question constantly asked as to the final effect upon wages of woman's entrance into public life, this question usually shaping itself under three heads: —

1. Why are they in the field?

2. How does their work compare in efficiency with that of men?

3. What is likely to be the final effect on wage of their entrance into active life?

The first phase has already had full answer in the general survey of trades and their rise and growth. As to the second, personal observation, long continued and minute, added to the very full knowledge to be obtained from the reports of the various State bureaus of labor, goes to prove beyond question that, given the same grade of intelligence, the work of women is fully equal to that of men. Descending in the scale to untrained labor in all its forms, the woman is at times of less value than the man. The Knights of Labor, however, settled definitely that this was seldom the case, and in their constitution demanded equal pay for equal work. For both sexes machinery is more and more superseding the labor of each; and as women and children are quite capable of running much of it, this fact, of course, brings the general wage to their standard. This, added to various physiological and social reasons, makes woman often a less dependable worker than man, and tends to keep wages at a minimum.

As to the final effect on wages, I regard the whole aspect of things as purely transitional, and must answer from personal conviction in the matter.

The entire movement appears to me a part of the natural evolution from barbaric law and restriction, and a necessary demonstration of the spiritual equality of the sexes. I regard it also as the nurse and developer of many small virtues in which women are especially deficient, — punctuality, unvarying quality of work, a sense of business honor and of personal fidelity, each to all and all to each. But I cannot feel that it is a permanent state, or that when the essential has been accomplished women will have the same need or the same desire that now rules. I believe that wages must necessarily fluctuate and tend to the mere point of subsistence when either child labor or the lowest grade of woman's labor exists, and that the only way out of the complications we face is in an alteration of ideals. Statistics and general reports show the demoralization of family life where such work goes on, and the fact that in the long run the workman loses rather than gains where his family share his labor.

The lowering of wage may be considered, then, as in one sense remedial, and the present state of things as in part the mere action of inevitable and inescapable law. But it is impossible to make this plain in present limits. Having passed through every stage of feeling,—sick pity, burning indignation, and tempestuous desire for instant action,—I have come at last to regard all as our education in justice and a demand for training in such wise as shall render unskilled labor more and more impossible. So long as it exists, however, I see no outlook but the fluctuating and uncertain wage, the natural result of the existence of the lowest order of workers.

For them as for us it is the development of the individual from the mass that is the chief end of any real civilization. No Utopias of any past or present can bring this at once.

> "Each man to himself and each woman to herself, such is the word of the past and the present, and the true word of immortality."

> "No one can acquire for another, not one;

> No one can grow for another, not one."

Despair might easily be the outcome of a first glance at these conditions; but the stir at all points is assurance of a better day to come.

Legislation can do much. The appointment of women inspectors, lately brought about for New York, is imperative at all points, since women will tell women the evils they would never mention to men. Law can also demand decent sanitary conditions, and affix a penalty for every violation. Beyond this, and the awakening of the public conscience as to what is owed the honest worker, little can be said.

Enlightenment, a better chance at every point for the struggling mass, — that is the work for each and all of them, and for those who would aid the constant demand, and labor for justice in its largest sense and its most rigorous application. With justice on both sides, abuses die of pure inanition. The tenement-house system, every evil that hedges about special trades, every wrong born of cupidity and ignorance, and all base features of trade at its worst, end once for all, and we see the end and aim of the social life, whether for employer or employed.

A generation ago Mazzini wrote: —

> "The human soul, not the body, should be the starting-point of all our efforts, since the body without the soul is only a carcass, whilst the soul, wherever it is found free and holy, is sure to mould for itself such a body as its wants and vocation require."

It is this soul-moulding that is given chiefly into the hands of women. It is through them that the higher ideal of life, its purpose and its demands, is to be made known. No present scheme of general philanthropy can touch this need. It is growth in the human soul itself that will mean justice from the employer to each and every worker, and from the worker in equal measure to the employer; and this justice can be implanted in the child as certainly as many another virtue, into the knowledge and love of which we grow but slowly.

Never has deeper interest followed every movement for the understanding and bettering of conditions. Never was there stronger ground for hope that, in spite of the worst abuses existing, man's will is to join hands at last with natural evolution toward higher forms. Faith and hope alike find their assurance in the increasing sense of the solidarity of human kind, and the spirit of brotherhood more and more discernible, which, as it grows, must end all oppression, conscious and unconscious. The old days of darkness are dying. Man knows at last that —

> "Laying hands on another,
>
> To coin his labor and sweat,

He goes in pawn to his victim

For eternal years in debt;"

   and in knowing it, the first step is taken in the new life wherein all are brothers; and the law of love, slowly as it may work, ends forever the long conflict between employer and employed.

FOOTNOTES:

[49] Transactions of the National Association for the Promotion of Social Science, 1857, p. 554.

[50] July, 1893.

APPENDIX.

FACTORY INSPECTION LAW.

PASSED MAY 18, 1886; AMENDED MAY 25, 1887; AMENDED JUNE 15, 1889; AMENDED MAY 21, 1890; AMENDED MAY 18, 1892.

CHAPTER 409, LAWS OF 1886 (AS AMENDED BY CHAPTER 673, LAWS OF 1892).

An act to Regulate the Employment of Women and Children in Manufacturing Establishments, and to Provide for the Appointment of Inspectors to Enforce the Same.

The People of the State of New York, represented in Senate and Assembly, do enact as follows:

SECTION I. No person under eighteen years of age, and no woman under twenty-one years or age, employed in any manufacturing establishment, shall be required, permitted, or suffered to work therein more than sixty hours in any one week, or more than ten hours in any one day, unless for the purpose of making a shorter work-day on the last day of the week, nor more hours in any one week than will make an average of ten hours per day for the whole number of days in which such person or such woman shall so work during such week; and in no case shall any person under eighteen years of age, or any woman under twenty-one years of age, work in any such establishment after nine o'clock in the evening or before six o'clock in the morning of any day. Every person, firm, corporation, or company employing any person under eighteen years of age, or any woman under twenty-one years of age, in any manufacturing establishment, shall post and keep posted in a conspicuous place in every room where such help is employed, a printed notice stating the number of hours of labor per day required of such persons for each day of the week, and the number of hours of labor exacted or permitted to be performed by such persons shall not exceed the number of hours of labor so posted as being required. The time of beginning and ending the day's labor shall be the time stated in such notice; provided that such women under twenty-one and persons under eighteen years of age may begin after the time set for beginning, and stop before the time set in such notice for the stopping of the day's labor; but they shall not be permitted or required to perform any labor before the time stated on the notices as the time for beginning the day's labor, nor after the time stated upon the notices as the hour for ending the day's labor. The terms of the notice stating the hours of labor required shall not be changed after the beginning of labor on the first day of the week without the consent of the Factory Inspector, Assistant Factory Inspector, or a Deputy Factory Inspector. When, in order to make a shorter workday on the last day of the week, women under twenty-one and youths under eighteen years of age are to be required, permitted, or suffered to work more than ten hours in any one day, in a manufacturing establishment, it shall be the duty of the proprietor, agent, foreman, superintendent, or other person employing such persons, to notify the Factory Inspector, Assistant Factory Inspector, or a Deputy Factory Inspector, in charge of the district, in writing, of such intention, stating the number of hours of labor per day which it is proposed to permit or require, and the date upon which the necessity for such lengthened day's labor shall cease, and also again forward such notification when it shall actually have ceased. A record of the amount of over-time so worked, and of the days upon which it was performed, with the names of the employees who were thus required or permitted to work more than ten hours in any one day, shall be kept in the office of the manufacturing establishment, and produced upon the demand of any officer appointed to enforce the provisions of this act.

§ 2. No child under fourteen years of age shall be employed in any manufacturing establishment within this State. It shall be the duty of every person employing children to keep a register, in which shall be recorded the name, birthplace, age and place of residence of every person employed by him under the age of sixteen years; and it shall be unlawful for any proprietor, agent, foreman, or other person in or connected with a manufacturing establishment to hire or employ any child under the age of sixteen years to work therein without there is first provided and placed on file in the orifice an affidavit made by the parent or guardian, stating the age, date, and place of birth of said child; if said child have no parent or guardian, then such affidavit shall be made by the child, which affidavit shall be kept on file by the employer, and which said register and affidavit shall be produced for inspection on demand made by the Inspector, Assistant Inspector, or any of the deputies appointed under this act. There shall be posted conspicuously in every room where children under sixteen years of age are employed, a list of their names with their ages respectively. No child under the age of sixteen years shall be employed in any manufacturing establishment who cannot read and write simple sentences in the English language, except during the vacation of the public schools in the city or town where such minor lives. The Factory Inspector, Assistant Inspector, and Deputy Inspectors shall have power to demand a certificate of physical fitness from some regular physician, in the case of children who may seem physically unable to perform the labor at which they may be employed, and shall have power to prohibit the employment of any minor that cannot obtain such a certificate.

§ 3. No person, firm, or corporation shall employ or permit any child under the age of fifteen years to have the care, custody, management of, or to operate any elevator, or shall employ or permit any person under the age of eighteen years to have the care, custody, management, or operation of any elevator running at a speed of over two hundred feet a minute.

§ 4. It shall be the duty of the owner, agent, or lessee of any manufacturing establishment where there is any elevator, hoisting-shaft, or well-hole, to cause the same to be properly and substantially inclosed or secured, if in the opinion of the Factory Inspector, or of the Assistant Factory Inspector, or a Deputy Factory Inspector, unless disapproved by the Factory Inspector, it is necessary to protect the lives or limbs of those employed in such establishment. It shall also be the duty of the owner, agent, or lessee of each of such establishments to provide or cause to be provided, if, in the opinion of the Inspector, the safety of persons in or about the premises should require it, such proper trap or automatic doors, so fastened in or at all elevator ways as to form a substantial surface when closed, and so constructed as to open and close by action of the elevator in its passage, either ascending or descending, but the requirements of this section shall not apply to passenger elevators that are closed on all sides. The Factory Inspector, Assistant Factory Inspector, and Deputy Factory Inspectors may inspect the cables, gearing, or other apparatus of elevators in manufacturing establishments, and require that the same be kept in a safe condition.

§ 5. Proper and substantial hand-rails shall be provided on all stairways in manufacturing establishments, and where, in the opinion of the Factory Inspector, or of the Assistant Factory Inspector, or Deputy Factory Inspector, unless disapproved by the Factory Inspector, it is necessary, the steps of said stairs in all such establishments shall be substantially covered with rubber, securely fastened thereon, for the better safety of persons employed in said establishments. The stairs shall be properly screened at the sides and bottom, and all doors leading in or to such factory shall be so constructed as to open outwardly where practicable, and shall be neither locked, bolted, nor fastened during working-hours.

§ 6. If, in the opinion of the Factory Inspector, or of the Assistant Factory Inspector, or of a Deputy Factory Inspector, it is necessary to insure the safety of the persons employed in any manufacturing establishment, three or more stories in height, one or more fire-escapes, as may be deemed by the Factory Inspector as necessary and sufficient therefor, shall be provided on the outside of such establishment, connecting with each floor above the first, well fastened and secured and of sufficient strength, each of which fire-escapes shall have landings or balconies, not less than six feet in length and three feet in width, guarded by iron railings not less than three feet in height, and embracing at least two windows at each story and connecting with the interior by easily accessible and un-obstructed openings, and the balconies or landings shall be connected by iron stairs, not less than eighteen inches wide, the steps not to be less than six inches tread, placed at a proper slant, and protected by a well-secured hand-rail on both sides with a twelve-inch-wide drop-ladder from the lower platform reaching to the ground. Any other plan or style of fire-escape shall be sufficient, if approved by the Factory Inspector; but if not so approved, the Factory Inspector may notify the owner, proprietor, or lessee of such establishment or of the building in which such establishment is conducted, or the agent or superintendent or either of them, in writing, that any such other plan or style of fire-escape is not sufficient, and may, by an order in writing, served in like manner, require one or more fire-escapes, as he shall deem necessary and sufficient, to be provided for such establishment, at such locations and of such plan and style as shall be specified in such written order. Within twenty days after the service of such order, the number of fire-escapes required in such order for such establishment shall be provided therefor, each of which shall be either of the plan and style and in accordance with the specifications in said order required, or of the plan and style in this section above described and declared to be sufficient. The windows or doors to each fire-escape shall be of sufficient size, and be located as far as possible consistent with accessibility, from the stairways and elevator hatchways or openings, and the ladder thereof shall extend to the roof. Stationary stairs or ladders shall be provided on the inside of such establishment from the upper story to the roof, as a means of escape in case of fire.

§ 7. It shall be the duty of the owner, agent, superintendent, or other person having charge of such manufacturing establishment, or of any floor or part thereof, to report in writing to the Factory Inspector all accidents or injury done to any person in such factory, within forty-eight hours of the time of the accident, stating as fully as possible the extent and cause of such injury, and the place where the injured person has been sent, with such other information relative thereto as may be required by the Factory Inspector. The Factory Inspector or Assistant Factory Inspector and Deputy Factory Inspectors under the supervision of the Factory Inspector, are hereby authorized and empowered to fully investigate the causes of such accidents, and to require such precautions to be taken as will in their judgment prevent the recurrence of similar accidents.

§ 8. It shall be the duty of the owner of any manufacturing establishment, or his agents, superintendent, or other person in charge of the same, to furnish and supply, or cause to be furnished and supplied therein, in the discretion of the Factory Inspector, or of the Assistant Factory Inspector, or of a Deputy Factory Inspector, unless disapproved by the Factory Inspector, where machinery is used, belt-shifters or other safe mechanical contrivances, for the purpose of throwing on or off belts or pulleys; and wherever possible machinery therein shall be provided with loose pulleys; all vats, pans, saws, planers, cogs, gearing, belting, shafting, set-screws, and machinery of every description therein shall be properly guarded, and no person shall remove or make ineffective any safeguard around or attached to any planer, saw, belting, shafting or other machinery, or around any vat or pan, while the same is in use, unless for the purpose of immediately making repairs thereto, and all such safeguards shall be promptly replaced. By attaching thereto a notice to that effect, the use of any machinery may be prohibited by the Factory Inspector, Assistant Factory Inspector, or by a Deputy Factory Inspector, unless such notice is disapproved by the Factory Inspector, should such machinery be regarded as dangerous. Such notice must be signed by the Inspector who issues it, and shall only be removed after the required safeguards are provided, and the unsafe or dangerous machine shall not be used in the mean time. Exhaust fans of sufficient power shall be provided for the purpose of carrying off dust from emery wheels and grindstones, and dust-creating machinery therein. No person under eighteen years of age and no woman under twenty-one years of age shall be allowed to clean machinery while in motion.

§ 9. A suitable and proper washroom and water-closets shall be provided in each manufacturing establishment, and such water-closets shall be properly screened and ventilated, and be kept at all times in a clean condition; and if women or girls are employed in any such establishment, the water-closets used by them shall have separate approaches and be separate and apart from those used by men. All water-closets shall be kept free of obscene writing and marking. A dressing-room shall be provided for women and girls, when required by the Factory Inspector, in any manufacturing establishment in which women and girls are employed.

§ 10. Not less than sixty minutes shall be allowed for the noonday meal in any manufacturing establishment in this State. The Factory

Inspector, the Assistant Factory Inspector, or any Deputy Factory Inspector shall have power to issue written permits in special cases, allowing shorter meal-time at noon, and such permit must be conspicuously posted in the main entrance of the establishment, and such permit may be revoked at any time the Factory Inspector deems necessary, and shall only be given where good cause can be shown.

§ 11. The walls and ceilings of each workroom in every manufacturing establishment shall be lime-washed or painted, when in the opinion of the Factory Inspector, Assistant Factory Inspector, or of a Deputy Factory Inspector, unless disapproved of by the Factory Inspector, it shall be conducive to the health or cleanliness of the persons working therein.

§ 12. Any officer of the Factory Inspection Department, or other competent person designated for such purpose by the Factory Inspector, shall inspect any building used as a workshop or manufacturing establishment or anything attached thereto, located therein or connected therewith, outside of the cities of New York and Brooklyn, which has been represented to be unsafe or dangerous to life or limb. If it appears upon such inspection that the building or anything attached thereto, located therein or connected therewith is unsafe or dangerous to life or limb, the Factory Inspector shall order the same to be removed or rendered safe and secure; and if such notification be not complied with within a reasonable time, he shall prosecute whoever may be responsible for such delinquency.

§ 13. No room or rooms, apartment or apartments, in any tenement or dwelling-house, shall be used for the manufacture of coats, vests, trousers, knee-pants, overalls, cloaks, furs, fur-trimmings, fur-garments, shirts, purses, feathers, artificial flowers, or cigars, excepting by the immediate members of the family living therein. No person, firm, or corporation shall hire or employ any person to work in any one room or rooms, apartment or apartments, in any tenement or dwelling-house, or building in the rear of a tenement or dwelling-house, at making in whole or in part any coats, vests, trousers, knee-pants, fur, fur-trimmings, fur-garments, shirts, purses, feathers, artificial flowers, or cigars, without first obtaining a written permit from the Factory Inspector, Assistant Factory Inspector, or a

Deputy Factory Inspector, which permit may be revoked at any time the health of the community or of those employed therein may require it, and which permit shall not be granted until an inspection of such premises is made by the Factory Inspector, Assistant Factory Inspector, or a Deputy Factory Inspector, and the maximum number of persons allowed to be employed therein shall be stated in such permit. Such permit shall be framed and posted in a conspicuous place in the room or in one of the rooms to which it relates.

§ 14. Not less than two hundred and fifty cubic feet of air space shall be allowed for each person in any workroom where persons are employed during the hours between six o'clock in the morning and six o'clock in the evening, and not less than four hundred cubic feet of air space shall be provided for each person in any workroom where persons are employed between six o'clock in the evening and six o'clock in the morning. By a written permit the Factory Inspector, Assistant Factory Inspector, or a Deputy Factory Inspector, with the consent of the Factory Inspector, may allow persons to be employed in a room where there are less than four hundred cubic feet of air space for each person employed between six o'clock in the evening and six o'clock in the morning, provided such room is lighted by electricity at all times during such hours while persons are employed therein. There shall be sufficient means of ventilation provided in each workroom of every manufacturing establishment; and the Factory Inspector, Assistant Factory Inspector, and Deputy Factory Inspectors, under the direction of the Factory Inspector, shall notify the owner, agent, or lessee, in writing, to provide, or cause to be provided, ample and proper means of ventilating such workroom, and shall prosecute such owner, agent, or lessee, if such notification be not complied with within twenty days of the service of such notice.

§ 15. Upon the expiration of the term of office of the present Factory Inspector, and upon the expiration of the term of office of each of his successors, the Governor shall, by and with the advice and consent of the Senate, appoint a Factory Inspector; and upon the expiration of the term of office of the present Assistant Factory Inspector, and upon the expiration of the term of office of each of his successors, the Governor shall, by and with the advice and consent of the Senate, appoint an Assistant Factory Inspector. Each Factory

Inspector and Assistant Factory Inspector shall hold over and continue in office, after the expiration of his term of office, until his successor shall be appointed and qualified. The Factory Inspector is hereby authorized to appoint from time to time not exceeding sixteen persons to be Deputy Factory Inspectors, not more than eight of whom shall be women; and he shall have power to remove the same at any time. The term of office of the Factory Inspector and of the Assistant Factory Inspector shall be three years each. Annual salaries shall be paid in equal monthly instalments, as follows: To the Factory Inspector, three thousand dollars; to the Assistant Factory Inspector, two thousand five hundred dollars; to each Deputy Factory Inspector, one thousand two hundred dollars. All necessary travelling and other expenses incurred by the Factory Inspector, Assistant Factory Inspector, and the Deputy Factory Inspectors in the discharge of their duties shall be paid monthly by the Treasurer upon the warrant of the Comptroller, issued upon proper vouchers therefor. A sub-office may be opened in the city of New York at an expense of not more than one thousand five hundred dollars a year. The reasonable necessary travelling and other expenses of the Deputy Factory Inspectors while engaged in the performance of their duties shall be paid upon vouchers approved by the Factory Inspector and audited by the Comptroller.

§ 16. It shall be the duty of the Factory Inspector, and the Assistant Factory Inspector, and of each of the Deputy Factory Inspectors under the supervision and direction of the Factory Inspector, to cause this act to be enforced, and to cause all violators of this act to be prosecuted; and for that purpose they and each of them are hereby empowered to visit and inspect at all reasonable hours, and as often as shall be practicable and necessary, all manufacturing establishments in this State. It shall be unlawful for any person to interfere with, obstruct, or hinder, by force or otherwise, any officer appointed to enforce the provisions of this act, while in the performance of his or her duties, or to refuse to properly answer questions asked by such officer with reference to any of the provisions hereof. The Factory Inspector may divide the State into districts, and assign one or more Deputy Factory Inspectors to each district, and transfer them from one district to another as the best interests of the State may, in his judgment, require. Any Deputy Factory Inspector may be appointed to act as Clerk in the main office of the Factory Inspector, which shall be furnished in the Capitol, and set apart for the use of the Factory Inspector. The Assistant Factory Inspector and Deputy Factory Inspectors shall make reports to the Factory Inspector from time to time, as may be required by the Factory Inspector, and the Factory Inspector shall make an annual report to the Legislature during the month of January of each year. The Factory Inspector, Assistant Factory Inspector, and each Deputy Factory Inspector shall have the same powers as a Notary Public to administer oaths and take affidavits in matters connected with the enforcement of the provisions of this act.

§ 17. The District Attorney of any county of this State is hereby authorized, upon the request of the Factory Inspector, Assistant Factory Inspector, or of a Deputy Factory Inspector, or of any other person of full age, to commence and prosecute to termination before any Recorder, Police Justice, or court of record, in the name of the people of the State, actions or proceedings against any person or persons reported to him to have violated the provisions of this act.

§ 18. The words "manufacturing establishment," wherever used in this act, shall be construed to mean any mill, factory, or workshop, where one or more persons are employed at labor.

§ 19. A copy of this act shall be conspicuously posted and kept posted in each workroom of every manufacturing establishment in this State.

§ 20. Any person who violates or omits to comply with any of the provisions of this act, or who suffers or permits any child to be employed in violation of its provisions, shall be deemed guilty of a misdemeanor, and on conviction shall be punished by a fine of not less than twenty nor more than fifty dollars for the first offence, and not more than one hundred dollars for the second offence, or imprisonment for not more than ten days, and for the third offence a fine of not less than two hundred and fifty dollars, and not more than thirty days' imprisonment.

§ 21. All acts and parts of acts inconsistent with the provisions of this act are hereby repealed.

§ 22. This act shall take effect immediately.

AUTHORITIES CONSULTED IN PREPARING THIS BOOK.

United States Census, from 1790 to 1880 inclusive.

Reports of the State Bureaus of Labor Statistics as follows: —

> Maine, 1889.
> Massachusetts, 1870 to 1889 inclusive.
> Connecticut, 1881.
> Rhode Island, 1889.
> New York, 1885.
> New Jersey, 1885, 1886, and 1889.
> Iowa, 1887 and 1889.
> Kansas, 1889.
> Wisconsin, 1883-84 and 1887.
> Colorado, 1889.
> Minnesota, 1889.
> California, 1888.
> Nebraska, 1887-90.
> Michigan, 1892.

Reports of the Factory Inspectors for various States.

Working Women in Large Cities: Report of the United States Department of Labor, Washington, D.C., 1889.

The Labor Movement in America. By Richard T. Ely. Thomas Y. Crowell & Co., New York.

The Wages Question: A Treatise on Wages and the Wages Class. By Francis A. Walker. Henry Holt & Co., New York.

The Labor Problem. Edited by W.E. Barnes. Harper & Brothers, New York.

On Labor. By W.T. Thornton. Macmillan & Co., London, 1869.

Profit-Sharing between Employer and Employed. By N.P. Gilman. Houghton, Mifflin, & Co., Boston.

Sharing the Profits. By Mary Whiton Calkins, A.M. Ginn & Co., Boston.

Artisans and Machinery. By P. Gaskell. London, 1836.

Condition of the Laboring Classes in England. By F. Engel. Leipzig and New York.

Ansichten der Volkswirthschaft aus dem geschicht. Standpunkte. By Wilhelm Roscher.

Various Reports of Commissioners appointed to inquire into the working of the Factory Acts in England.

Le Travail des Femmes au XIX. Siècle. By Paul Leroy-Beaulieu. Paris, 1870.

London Labor and the London Poor. By Henry Mayhew. Charles Griffen & Co., London.

The Industrial Revolution. By Arnold Toynbee. London.

The Philosophy of Wealth. By John B. Clark. Ginn & Co., Boston.

Economic Writings of Emil de Lavelaye.

Lalor's Cyclopedia of Political Science.

Various Treatises on Political Economy. Adam Smith, John Stuart Mill, Senior, Cairnes, Ely, Perry, Walker, etc.

Prisoners of Poverty. By Helen Campbell. Roberts Bros., Boston.

Applied Christianity. By Washington Gladden. Houghton, Mifflin, & Co., Boston.

Life and Work of the Earl of Shaftesbury, London. Read for Factory Inspection and Legislation.

Problems of To-Day. By Richard T. Ely. T.Y. Crowell & Co., New York.

Social Studies. By the Rev. R. Heber Newton. G.P. Putnam's Son, New York.

Social Problems. By Henry George.

Studies in Modern Socialism. By Edwin Brown, D.D. Appleton & Co., New York.

Dynamic Sociology. By Lester F. Ward. D. Appleton & Co., New York.

Labor and Life of the People. Vols. 1 & 2: East London. By Charles Booth. Williams & Norgate, London, 1889 & 1892.

Thirty Years of Labor: 1859 to 1889. By T.V. Powderly.

Das Kapital. By Karl Marx.

How the Other Half Live. By Jacob Riis. Charles Scribner's Sons, New York.

General Reports and Review Articles on the questions involved.

BIBLIOGRAPHY OF WOMAN'S LABOR AND OF THE WOMAN QUESTION.

GERMANY.

Ausser den amtlichen Veröffentlichungen der verschiedenen Länder, über Berufs-und Bevölkerungstatistik vgl G. Schmoller, Thatsachen der Arbeitsteilung, Jahrb. f. Ges. und Berw. Bd 13, 1889.

Buchsenschutz, Besitz und Erwerb in griechischen Alterthum. Halle, 1869.

Franz Bernhoft, Ueber die Stellung der Frauen in Alterthum, Nord und Süd. Bd. 39, 1884.

K. Weinhold, Die deutschen Frauen im Mittelalter, 2 Auflage. Wien, 1882.

Norrenberg, Frauenarbeit und Arbeiterinnenziehung in deutscher Vorzeit. Köln, 1780.

Stahl, Das deutsche Handwerk. Giessen, 1874.

Carl Bücher, Die Frauenfrage im Mittelalter. Tübingen, 1882.

Stieda, Litteratur, heutige Zustände und Entstehung der deutschen Hausindustrie. Leipzig, 1889. [Schr. d. Ver. f. Soz. Bd. 39.]

Ad. Held, Zwei Bücher zur socialen Geschichte Englands. Leipzig, 1848.

Fr. Engels, Die Lage der arbeitenden Klasse in England. 2 Ausgabe. Leipzig, 1848.

Karl Marx, Das Kapital, Band 1, 2 Auflage. Hamburg, 1872.

Max Schippel, Das moderne Elend und die moderne Uebervölkerung. Stuttgart, 1886.

Von Scherzer, Weltindustrien. Leipzig, 1880.

Ettore Friedlander, Die Frage der Frauen-und Kinderarbeit, deutsch von Fleischer. Forbach, 1887.

Ergebnisse der über die Frauen-und Kinderarbeit in den Fabriken auf Beschluss des Bundesraths angestellten Erhebungen, zusammengestellt im Reichskanzleramt. Berlin, 1877.

W. Stieda, Deutschlands sozialstatistische Erhebungen im Jahre 1876. Jahrb. f. Ges. und Verw. R.F. Bd. 1, 1877.

Eine Enquete über Frauen-und Kinderarbeit in der deutsche Flachs-und Leinenindustrie. Arbeiterfreund, Jahrg. 12, 1874.

Reichsenquete über die Baumwoll-und Leinenindustrie, 1878-79.

Stenograph, Protokolle des Bundesrathes, 1878-79.

Worishoffer, Die soziale Lage der Cigarrenarbeiter im Grossherzogthum Baden. Karlsruhe, 1890.

Amtliche Mittheilungen aus den Jahresberichten der mit Beaufsichtigung der Fabriken betrauten Beamten, Jahrg. 1-14. Berlin, 1877-90.

Elster, Die Fabrikinspektionsberichte, und die Arbeiterschutzgesetzgebung in Deutschland. Jahrb. f. Nat. R.F. Bd. 11. 1885.

P. Kollmann, Die gewerbliche Entfaltung im deutschen Reiche. Jahrb. f. Ges. und Verw. R.F., Bd. 11 und 12. 1888-89.

Kuno Frankenstein, Die Lage der Arbeiterinnen in den deutschen Grossstadten, ebenda Bd. 12. 1888.

Eug. Kämpfe, Die Lage der industriellthätigen Arbeiterinnen in Deutschland. Leipzig, 1889.

O. Pache, Unsere Arbeiterfrauen. Leipzig, 1880.

Bericht der Gewerbeordnungscommission des Reichstages, 7 Legislaturperiode, 1 Session, 1890-91, Sammlung d. Drucksachen des

Reichstages, 7 Legislaturperiode, 1 Session 1887, Bd. 2, Berlin, 1887, Nr. 83.

Karl Kaerger, Die Sachsgangerei, Landw. Jahrb. Bd. 13. 1890.

Hirschberg, Lohne der Arbeiterinnen in Berlin. Jahrb. f. Nat. Bd. 13. 1886.

Herkner, Die belgische Arbeiterenquete und ihre sozialpolitischen Resultate. Archiv f. soz. Ges. und Staat, Bd. 1. 1888.

Derselbe, Die oberelsassische Baumwollindustrie und ihre Arbeiter. Strassburg, 1887.

Ruhland, Der achtstundige Arbeitstag und die Arbeitschutzgesetzgebung Australiens. Zeitschr. f.d. ges. Staatsgewissenschaft, Bd. 47. 1891.

v. Studnitz, Amerikanische Arbeitverhältnisse. Leipzig, 1879.

Douai, Die Lage der Lohnarbeiter in Amerika, in Tenner, Amerika. Berlin und New York, 1884.

Hirt, Die gewerbliche Thätigkeit der Frauen von hygienischen Standpunkte aus. Breslau und Leipzig, 1887.

Derselbe, Frauenarbeit in Fabriken, in Hirth's Ann. 1875.

Schuler und Burkhardt, Untersuchungen über die Gesundheitsverhältnisse der Fabrikbevölkerung in der Schweiz. Aarau, 1889.

Schonlank, Die Further Quecksilber-Spiegelbelege. Stuttgart, 1888.

Pfieffer, Die proletarische und criminelle Säuglingssterblichkeit Jahrb. f. Nat. N.F. Bd. 4. 1882.

John Stuart Mill, The Subjection of Women. London, 1869; 4 Aufl., 1878, übersetzt von Jenny Hirsch, v.d. Hörigkeit der Frau, 2 Aufl., Berlin 1872, nebst einem Vorbericht über den Stand der Frauenfrage, übersetzt von Ludwig Stockman, 3 Aufl. Stuttgart, 1892.

Die Frau und die Sozialismus, 8 Aufl. Stuttgart, 1891.

v. Raumer, Die Frau und die Sozialdemokratie. Berlin, 1884.

Georg Hannsen, Die drei Bevölkerungsstufen, [111,7: Das Weib im Bevölkerungsstrom]. München, 1889.

Karoline Norton, Die Frauen in England unter dem Gesetz unseres Jahrhunderts. A.D. Engl. Berlin, 1855.

Rubinu und Westergaard, Statistik der Ehen auf Grund der sozialen Gliederung. Jena, 1889.

Lette, Denkschrift über die Eröffnung neuer und die Verbesserung bisheriger Erwerbsquellen für das weibliche Geschlecht. Arbeiterfreund, Jahrb. 1865. Auszug aus dem Protokoll der Sitzung des Vorstandes und Ausschusses des Zent.-Ver. in Preussen für das Wohl der arbeitenden Klasse, nebst Lettes Votum und Promemoria und andere Materialen, ebenda.

Gust. Eberty, Geschichte der Bestrebungen für das Wohl der arbeitenden Frauen in England, ebenda.

Luisa Otto, Das Recht der Frauen auf Erwerb. Hamburg, 1868.

Otto August, Die soziale Lage auf dem Gebiete der Frauen. Hamburg, 1868.

v. Sybel, Ueber die Emanzipation der Frauen. Bonn, 1860.

Karl Thomas Richter, Das Recht der Frauen auf Arbeit and die Organization der Frauenarbeit, 2 Aufl. Wien, 1869.

Schönberg, Die Frauenfrage. Basel, 1872.

Phil. v. Nathusius, Zur Frauenfrage. Halle, 1871.

Rob. König, Zur Charakteristik der Frauenfrage. Leipzig und Bielefeld, 1879.

Hedwig Dohm, Der Frauen Natur und Recht. Berlin, 1876. Dieselbe, Die wissenschaftliche Emancipation der Frau. Berlin, 1877.

Fanny Lewald, Für und wider die Frauen, 2 Aufl. Berlin, 1875.

Franz von Holzendorff, Die Verbesserung in der gesellschaftlichen und wirtschaftlichen Stellung der Frauen, 2 Aufl. Berlin, 1877.

Luisa Büchner, Ueber die Frauenemanzipation. Dorpat, 1877.

J. Pierstorff, Frauenfrage und Frauenbewegung. Göttingen, 1879.

Sophie v. Hardenburg, Zur Frauenfrage. Leipzig, 1883.

Laas, Zur Frauenfrage. Berlin, 1883.

Lor. v. Stein, Die Frau auf dem Gebiete der Nationalökonomie, 6 Aufl. Stuttgart, 1886. Derselbe, Die Frau auf dem sozialen Gebiete. Stuttgart, 1880.

Mathilde Reichart Stromberg, Frauenrecht und Frauenpflicht, 3 Aufl. Leipzig, 1883.

F.L. Warneck, Ehret die Frauen, 2 Aufl. Leipzig, 1882.

Dorothea Christina Erxleben, [geb. Leporin,] Gründliche Untersuchen der Ursachen, die das weibliche Geschlecht von Studieren abhalten, darin deren Unerheblichkeit gezeiget, und wie möglich, nöthig und nützlich es sei, dieses Geschlecht der Gelehrtheit sich befleissige, umständlich dargelegt we wird. Berlin, 1742. Dieselbe, Vernünftige Gedanken vom Studieren des Schönen Geschlechts. Frankfurt und Leipzig, 1749.

Victor Böhmert, Das Studium der Frauen in besonderer Rücksicht auf das Studium der Medizin. Leipzig, 1872. Derselbe, Das Frauenstudium nach den Erfahrungen an der Züricher Universität. Arbeiterfreund, Bd. 12. 1874.

Hermann, Die Frauenstudien und die Interessen der Hochschule Zurich. Zurich, 1872.

Gneist, Ueber gemeinschaftliche Schulen für Knaben und Mädchen und über die Universitätsbildung der Frauen nach den neueren Erfahrungen in den nordamerikanischen Freistaaten. Arbeiterfreund, Jahrg. 12. 1874.

v. Scheel, Frauenfrage und Frauenstudium. Jahrb. f. Nat., Bd. 22, 1874.

Eug. Dühring, Weg zur höheren Berufsbildung der Frauen, 2 Aufl. Leipzig, 1885.

Helene Lange, Frauen Bildung. Berlin, 1889.

Zehender, Ueber den Beruf der Frauen zum Studium und zur praktischen Ausübung der Medezin durch die Frauen. München, 1877.

Ludwig Schwerin, Die Zulassung der Frauen zur Ausübung des artzlichen Berufs. Berlin, 1870.

Mathilde Weber, Aerztinnen für Frauenkrankheiten, eine ethische und sanitäre Nothwendigkeit, 4 Aufl. Tübingen, 1889.

Waldeyer, Das Studium der Medizin und die Frauen. Tagebl. der 61. Versammlung deutscher Naturforscher und Artzerei in Köln, v. 18, 23, No. 1878, wissenschaftl. Theil. Köln, 1889.

O. Heyfelder, Die medizinischen Frauenkurse von Petersburg. Unsere Zeit, 1887, 11.

Karl Breul, Die Frauencolleges der Universität Cambridge, England. Preuss. Jahrb., Jahrg. 1891, Heft 1.

Die Entstehung und Entwickelung der gewerblichen Fortbildungsschulen und Frauenarbeitsschulen in Würtemberg; herausgegeben von der Königlichen Commission für die gewerblichen Fortbildungsschulen, 2 Aufl. Stuttgart, 1889.

Galle und Kamp, Die hauswirthschaftliche Unterweisung armer Mädchen. Wiesbaden, 1889; Neue Folge, Wiesbaden, 1889. Die hauswirthschaftliche Unterricht armer Mädchen in Deutschland. Schr. d. Ver. f. Armenpflege und Wohlthätigkeit, Heft 12. Leipzig, 1889.

Lina Morgenstern, Allgemeiner Frauenkalender für 1885, 1886, und 1887. Berlin.

Luise Otto Peters, Das erste Vierteljahrhundert des Allgemeinen deutschen Frauenvereins. Leipzig, 1890.

Jenny Hirsch, Geschichte der 25-jahrigen Wirksamkeit [1886-91] des Lettevereins. [Festschrift.] Berlin, 1891.

Amelie Sohr, Frauenarbeit in der Armen-und Krankenpflege daheim und im Auslande. Berlin, 1882.

Ed. Gauer, Die höhere Mädchenschule und die Lehrerinnenfrage. Berlin, 1878.

Spyri, Die Betheiligung des weiblichen Geschlechts am öffentlichen Unterricht in der Schweiz. Sep.-Abdr. der schweizer. Zeitschrift f. Gemeinnützigkeit, Jahrg. 1873, Zurich.

Rüdinger, Vorläufige Mittheilung über die Unterschiede der Grosshirnwindungen nach dem Geschlecht, Beiträge zur Anthropologie und Urgeschichte Bayerns, Bd. 1, 1887.

J. Pierstorff, Litteratur zur Frauenfrage. Jahrb. f. Nat. N.F. Bd. 7. 1883.

Während des Druckes erschienen:

Ed. von Hartmann, Die Jungfernfrage, Gegenwart 1891, Nr. 34 und 35.

W. Stieda, Frauenarbeit. Jahrb. f. Nat., Dritte Folge, 11, 2, 1891.

BIBLIOGRAPHY OF FRENCH LITERATURE ON THE WOMAN QUESTION AND THAT OF WOMAN'S LABOR.

Levasseur, Histoire des classes ouvrières depuis 1788. Paris, 1867.

Paul Leroy-Beaulieu, Le travail des femmes au XIX. siècle. Paris, 1873.

Jules Simon, L'ouvrière, 2me édition. Paris, 1870.

Villermé, Tableau de l'état physique et moral des ouvriers employés dans les manufactures de coton, de laine et de soie. Paris, 1840.

Kuborn, Rapport sur l'enquête faite au nom de l'académie royale de medicine de Belgique par la commission chargée d'étudier la question de l'emploi des femmes dans les travaux souterrains des mines. Bruxelles, 1868. Documents nouveaux relatifs au travail des femmes et des enfants dans les manufactures, les mines, etc., etc. Bruxelles, 1874.

Condorcet, Lettres d'un bourgeois de New Haven à un citoyen de Virginie, 1787. OEuvres complètes, Brunswick, 1804. The same, Sur l'admission des femmes au droit de cité. Journal de la société de 1789, v. 3, VII. 1790.

Laboulaye, Recherches sur la condition civile et politique des femmes depuis les Romains jusqu'à nos jours. Paris, 1843.

Legouvé, Histoire morale de la femme. Paris, 1848; 4me édition, 1884.

Michelet, La femme. Paris, 1860.

Proudhon, La justice dans l'église et dans la révolution, 1858. Oeuvres anciennes, Paris, 1868-76. Tome 22-26.

Jenny d'Hericourt, La femme affranchie. Bruxelles, 1860.

Juliette Lamber, Idées antiproudhoniennes sur l'amour, la femme et le mariage, 2me édition. Paris, 1862.

Leon Giraud, Essai sur la condition de la femme en Europe et en Amérique. Paris, 1883.

Eugène Pelletan, La famille. La mère. Paris, 1865.

Actes du Congrès international des droits des femmes. Paris, 1878.

Comte de Franqueville, Les droits des femmes en Angleterre, Compte rendu de l'Académie des sciences morales et politiques. Paris, 1891.

ENGLISH BIBLIOGRAPHY.

Working Women in Large Cities, 4th annual Report of the Commission of Labor. Washington, 1878.

Theodore Stanton, The Woman Question in Europe. London, 1884.

Helen Campbell, Prisoners of Poverty, 1887. Prisoners of Poverty Abroad, 1889.

Woman's Work in America, edited by Annie Nathan Meyer. New York, 1891.

Sophia Jex-Blake, Medical Women. Edinburgh, 1871.

A. Huntley, Women and Medicine. London, 1886.

John Stuart Mill, Subjection of Women. London, 1869.

Eliza W. Farnham, Woman and her Era. New York, 1869.

Lester F. Ward, Dynamic Sociology, vol. i. pp. 597-664.

Maria S. Child, History and Condition of Women in various Ages and Nations. Boston, 1840.